SPORTS SCIENCE

THE SCIENCE OF BASEBALL

AMY B. ROGERS

ROSEN PUBLISHING

Published in 2026 by The Rosen Publishing Group, Inc.
2544 Clinton Street, Buffalo, NY 14224

Portions of this work were originally authored by Lizabeth Hardman and published as *Baseball.* All new material this edition authored by Amy B. Rogers

Designer: Rachel Rising
Editor: Jill Keppeler

Names: Rogers, Amy B.
Title: The science of baseball / Amy B. Rogers.
Description: Buffalo, NY : Rosen Publishing, 2026. | Series: Sports science | Includes glossary and index.
Identifiers: ISBN 9781499479362 (pbk.) | ISBN 9781499479379 (library bound) | ISBN 9781499479386 (ebook)
Subjects: LCSH: Baseball--Juvenile literature. | Sports sciences--Juvenile literature.
Classification: LCC GV867.5 R64 2026 | DDC 796.357--dc23

Manufactured in the United States of America

CPSIA Compliance Information: Batch #CSRYA26. For further information, contact Rosen Publishing at 1-800-237-9932.

CONTENTS

FOREWORD

The way that high-caliber athletes perform can seem unbelievable. To many people watching in the stands or from home, their feats may seem unreal—as unlikely as learning to fly. Even regular players and participants in these sports may stare in awe, feeling like they can never reach those heights.

However, the laws of nature are still the law and still unbreakable, and once you learn more about how the science behind these sports works, they're in some ways even more amazing. Peak athletes use the laws of nature and science to achieve their unbelievable feats, and understanding these laws can give you an even greater appreciation for their achievements. Science makes the incredible understandable and the seemingly unreal real. Rather than ruining an appreciation for sports, it can deepen our understanding and increase our awe.

In these books, readers can learn more about the scientific ideas behind athletic achievements, from the simplest hit in baseball to the most amazing gymnastics flip. Physics principles such as gravity, friction and drag, and Newton's laws of motion can all be applied to sports—and this means all sports, including swimming, football, track, and lacrosse. Readers will also learn about other scientific aspects of sports, including the whys and hows of athletic training, the principles of sports medicine, and the advances in technology that will affect these fields for years to come. Understanding the background can help young athletes better train for their sport, avoid injury, and better care for injuries when they do happen.

These principles and ideas are presented in clear,

understandable ways, with relatable and clear examples, including quotes from those who play and participate in the sports, those who coach and help them, and those who study the science behind it all. Graphic tools including charts and diagrams help present these concepts, with a glossary and other resources added to assist in reader curiosity.

While science and its basic principles may seem unrelatable and unable to apply to real life, this set will give readers a reason (or many reasons) to question that assessment. Science is real, and it affects every aspect of our lives, even the things we do and watch for the sheer fun of it.

Sports and science are intrinsically intertwined. The basic principles of sports are the basic laws of science, and understanding one side will help you understand the other better. This is true for sports fans and young scientists alike!

Baseball players of all ages and skill levels use the laws of science to accomplish amazing feats!

CHAPTER ONE

A NATIONAL PASTIME

Opening Day! For more than 100 years, those two words have had a magic to them that only baseball fans understand. The first day of the regular season of Major League Baseball (MLB) is a sign of spring and, to some, even a symbol of rebirth. The slate is clean; anyone (at least technically) can go on to win it all. Is it, then, any surprise that some people and families see it as an annual rite of passage to turn on the TV (or head out to the ballpark) on that day?

That said, baseball is a sport that, in recent years, has faded to the background of the American consciousness. Football and basketball dominate the modern sports fan's attention, and the median age of a baseball ticket buyer in 2024 was 45. (Though this is a drop from 10 years before.) Some people believe baseball is not interesting to younger people, but the truth is that the game can be very exciting to people who understand how it works. Baseball is a game filled with angles and different perspectives, and many of those are now understood and well-examined.

As Jon Bois wrote for the website SB Nation in "There Is No Future of Baseball," the game has evolved:

> *Baseball has no single inventor, it was built across generations. Kids in 18th-century England played a game in which they stood over a thing they called "home plate" and were given three tries to hit a ball. The sport evolved gradually before exploding in popularity during the Civil War, which, for all its disaster and sorrow, was largely*

composed of absolute boredom. Otherwise-idle soldiers in camps flocked to baseball in the absence of anything else in the world to do.

Since then, a few minor recalibrations have been made—raising and lowering of the mound, contraction and expansion of outfield fences, a brief 1887 experiment with a fourth strike—but baseball's chassis [structure] has remained unchanged.[1]

Still, baseball is essential to American culture and its sports consciousness. The people who love baseball really love it, and they generally do for the rest of their lives. "The game gets inside you," said Eric Wedge, who has served as a manager with the Cleveland Indians and Seattle Mariners. "It becomes a part of who you are, and you don't know anything different. It's just something you feel passionate about. If you really feel that strong about something and you feel something that special, it's really hard to put it into words. For me, the love of the game is a given. It's been the one constant that I've known, for as far back as I can remember."[2]

PART OF THE FABRIC

Despite the ebb and flow of interest, it's still a definite fact that baseball is part of U.S. culture and has been for a very long time. Essayist Gerald Early said, "I think that there are only three things that America will be known for two thousand years from now when they study this civilization: the Constitution, jazz music, and baseball."[3] Dozens of movies have been made about baseball. Countless songs and poems have been written about the game, including "Take Me Out to the Ballgame" and "Casey at the Bat."

Dozens of baseball expressions have become part of everyday American language. As Tristram Potter Coffin observed in *The Old Ball Game*, "The true test comes in the fact that old ladies who have never been to the ballpark, coquettes [young ladies] who don't know or care who's on first, men who think athletics begin and end with a pair of goal posts still know and use a great deal of baseball-derived terminology."[4]

Here are a few examples: If people do something wrong, they have "dropped the ball," but if they do something right, they are "still in the game." If they do it right every time, they are "batting a thousand." Most people have "gone to bat in a pinch" for friends who have "two strikes against them." If people are waiting their turn at something, they are "on deck." If they are estimating something, they might give a "ballpark figure." When making important plans, people always try to "cover all the bases." Something you know a lot about is "in your wheelhouse," a term for a hitter's power zone.

IN THE BEG-INNING

Although there are many different versions of bat-and-ball games around the world, the game Americans call baseball evolved mostly from early folk games played in England. The first known mention of baseball in print appears in a book called *A Little Pretty Pocket-Book*, published in England in 1744. The book contains a short poem called "Base-Ball," accompanied by a picture of people playing a game of stoolball, a 14th-century English folk game. In stoolball, a batter stood in front of a target, often a tree stump or a stool turned upside down. The pitcher threw the ball at the target, and the batter tried to defend the target by hitting the ball away with either a bat or a bare hand. If the ball hit the stool, the

The game of cricket likely led, at least in part, to baseball. It's still very popular in some parts of the world today.

ON BASE There are more than 100 slang words for "hit," such as "blooper," "Texas Leaguer," "bleeder," "nibbler," "scratch," "seeing eye," and "squib."

batter was out. In some versions, no running was involved. In others, the batter might run between two stools or around several stools.

Cricket is a very old game that is still popular in England and also believed to have contributed to the development of baseball. In cricket, two runners stand at either end of a rectangle called the "pitch," which is 58 feet (17.68 m) long. Each runner stands next to a wicket—three poles stuck close together in the ground, topped by two wooden pieces called "bails." The wicket serves as a target, as in stoolball. One runner is the striker, or batsman. A bowler, or pitcher, throws the ball as hard as possible toward the striker. When the striker hits the ball, both runners run to the other end of the pitch, which scores a run. Meanwhile, the fielders try to catch the ball and throw it in to break the wicket before the runner can get back to it.

Rounders is another English game that is related to baseball, except that the pitcher and the batter are on the same team, runners run clockwise, the batter is out whether the ball is caught on the fly or on a bounce, and runners are out if the fielder hits them with the ball. In the early 1800s, Americans played a version of rounders that they called town ball. In both games, if there are three strikes, the batter is out. Sound familiar?

WRITING THE RULES

People differ on baseball's ultimate origins. Some baseball historians believe baseball and town ball evolved separately from one another. Others believe baseball had nothing to do with either cricket or rounders, and that it is a purely American invention. One fact is certain, however: The first official rules for baseball were written in 1845 for a New York City baseball club called the Knickerbockers. They were called the "Knickerbocker Rules."

The man who wrote the Knickerbocker Rules was a New Yorker named Alexander J. Cartwright. Many people consider him the "Father of Baseball." In the late 1840s, Cartwright became caught up in the California Gold Rush. As he traveled West, he introduced his version of the game to many of the cities through which he passed. In 1953, the U.S. Congress officially declared him to be the true inventor of modern baseball, and he is in the Baseball Hall of Fame in Cooperstown, New York.

In 1846, the first organized game between two baseball clubs took place in Hoboken, New Jersey, between the Knickerbockers and the New York Nine. In 1857, the National Association of Base Ball Players (NABBP) was formed as the first organization to govern the rules of baseball. Sixteen ball clubs (early teams were called clubs) met and rewrote the Knickerbocker Rules. By 1865, more than 100 clubs belonged to the NABBP, and more than 400 had joined by 1867.

Baseball was beginning to catch on with the public, and clubs began to build their own parks, charge admission to the games,

Cy Young, shown here, was a pitcher in the early days of Major League Baseball, which officially formed in 1903.

The Cincinnati Red Stockings are shown just before they turned professional.

and pay their players. In 1869, the Cincinnati Red Stockings became the first fully professional baseball team, followed by the Boston Red Stockings in 1871.

In 1870, conflicts between professional and amateur ball clubs resulted in the formation of the National Association of Professional Base Ball Players (NAPBBP). The NAPBBP lasted until 1875, when the National League of Professional Base Ball Clubs was formed. The National League included only teams from larger cities that were more competitive and financially strong. It imposed rules that prevented players from going to other teams for more pay and required teams to play all scheduled games, even if they were out of the running for the league championship. At about this time, both organizations unofficially agreed to exclude Black players from professional baseball. Several Black players already on teams were dropped from the rosters.

Smaller regional baseball associations existing at the time formed the roots of today's minor league system. In 1900,

THE BLACK SOX SCANDAL

Chicago White Sox owner Charles Comiskey was one of the most despised owners in baseball. In 1919, the White Sox were the best team in baseball, but their players were also the lowest paid. Comiskey frequently made promises he never intended to keep. After promising pitcher Eddie Cicotte a $10,000 bonus if he won 30 games, Comiskey benched him after he won his 29th. He tried to make the players pay for laundering their uniforms, and, when they refused, he had the uniforms laundered and then fined the players.

These and other behaviors created resentment among the players, so several of them decided to "fix" the World Series that year—they would lose on purpose. The players deliberately made mistakes so the Cincinnati Reds would win the World Series. The White Sox would lose, and professional gamblers would make money by betting on the other team. Since the White Sox were heavily favored to win, betting against them would earn the gamblers a lot of money. The gamblers agreed to pay $100,000 to the players who participated in the fix.

The Reds won the World Series, but the unusually bad play by the White Sox did not go unnoticed. Rumors flew that the series had been fixed. In 1920, a grand jury was convened to investigate, but, after important evidence went missing, the players were found not guilty of fixing the games. However, because the reputation of baseball had been damaged, Federal Judge Kenesaw Mountain Landis, the first commissioner of baseball, banned eight White Sox players, including Shoeless Joe Jackson, from ever playing baseball again. A few of them tried to clear their names, but none of the eight were ever reinstated in Major League Baseball. The last of them died in 1975.

one of these minor leagues, the Western League, decided to challenge the National League's dominance and became the American League. It competed with the National League by luring players away with better contracts. In 1903, the American and National Leagues merged to form Major League Baseball.

Eventually, most minor league teams became associated with a major league team. Today, the minor leagues provide a place for younger players to earn a living while improving their skills,

ON BASE Joe Nuxhall was only 15 years old when he pitched part of a Major League game for the Cincinnati Reds in 1944.

with the hope of eventually moving up to a major league team. Most of these teams are based in smaller cities.

RESURRECTING THE GAME

During the first 20 years of the 1900s, baseball was a rather different game. These years were commonly known as the "dead ball era" in baseball. Games were low scoring, and batters played "small ball," focusing on singles and moving runners along basepaths by bunting and stealing bases. Despite power hitters such as Honus Wagner and Ty Cobb, home runs were rare, and pitchers dominated. One reason for this was that baseballs were expensive to make, so one ball might be used the entire game. By the end, it could be covered with mud, grass, and other substances such as spit and tobacco juice. Balls in this condition were hard to see and, thus, hard to hit out of the park. The dead ball era ended in 1920, mainly because of one rule change and one player.

In 1920, Cleveland Indians shortstop Ray Chapman was hit in the head by a pitch and died the next day. Because of this,

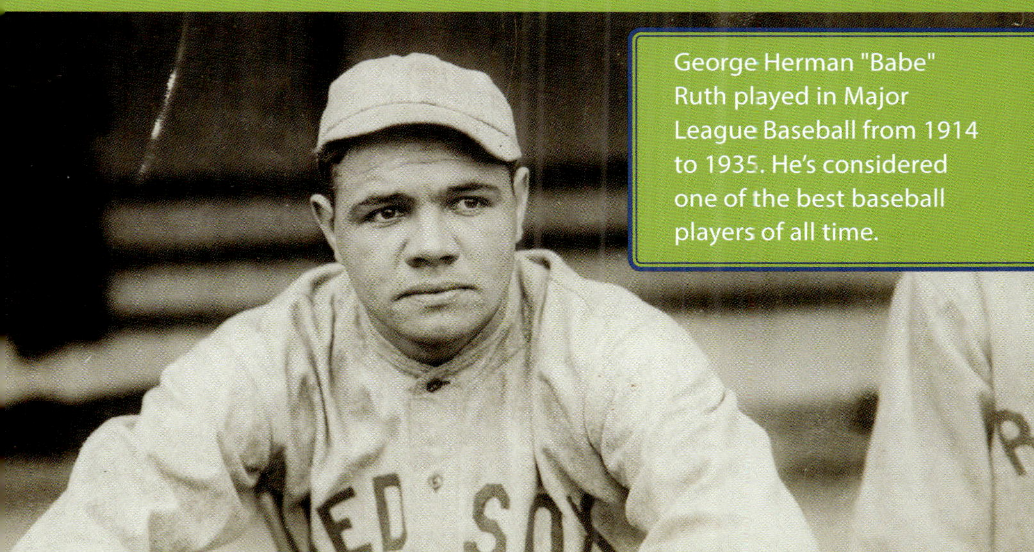

George Herman "Babe" Ruth played in Major League Baseball from 1914 to 1935. He's considered one of the best baseball players of all time.

THE ERA OF ALL-BLACK BASEBALL LEAGUES

By the late 1800s, in response to being excluded from Major League Baseball, Black Americans had formed their own professional teams. The first Black professional baseball team, the Babylon Black Panthers, was formed in 1885. White businessman Walter Cook sponsored them, and because the country of Cuba was on good terms with the United States at the time, he renamed the team the Cuban Giants, hoping to attract more white spectators.

In 1917, the United States entered World War I. The need for workers in the defense industry attracted a great number of Black southerners to the northern states. With a larger fan base, the push was on to start a new Black baseball league. In 1920, the Negro National League was formed with eight teams. The first league game was played on May 2, 1920. Other all-Black leagues formed as well, but largely due to the Great Depression, almost all of them had folded by the early 1930s. In 1933, a known gangster named Gus Greenlee decided to start a new seven-team league. He already owned a team that included two of the most famous Black players, Satchel Paige and Josh Gibson. He re-used the name Negro National League. In 1937, the Negro American League joined Greenlee's league. In 1942, they held the Negro League World Series.

After the major leagues became integrated in 1947, interest in all-Black leagues faded. Promising young Black players signed with MLB teams, and players who already had contracts with Negro League teams abandoned them for the majors. The Negro National League folded in 1948, followed by the Negro American League in 1958.

Major League Baseball instituted the rule that umpires must remove a ball from a game if it becomes dirty and hard to see. The ball is also replaced if the pitcher applies any substance to it, such as spit, that causes an "unnatural flight" through the air, or if it becomes scuffed or damaged. With the ball easier to see and with pitchers forbidden to alter the natural flight of the ball, batters hit more home runs.

While the change was made for safety's sake, the move was also a considerable physics lesson for MLB players. Pitchers had long known that doctoring, or altering, the ball with substances and scuffs made it move differently. Now, to make a ball curve or dip, pitchers had to either get more crafty with their skirting of the rules or learn to throw different pitches. The science behind baseball became much more important in the "live" ball era.

At about the same time, Boston Red Sox pitcher George Herman "Babe" Ruth was switched to the outfield so that he could bring his considerable hitting talent to the game every day instead of only every four days, because pitchers do not play every day. In his last season with the Red Sox, he hit 29 home runs. The next year, as a New York Yankee, he hit 54, and in 1921, he hit 59. In 1927, he hit 60 home runs—a record that lasted until 1961. The dead ball era was over.

Fans loved home runs, dubbed "the long ball." Clubs modified their parks to make home runs easier to hit, and teams lined up to sign "sluggers" who could hit home runs. Hitting, rather than pitching, came to dominate the game, and power hitters such as Babe Ruth, Rogers Hornsby, Lou Gehrig, Jimmie Foxx,

Jackie Robinson is in the Baseball Hall of Fame. He was the first Black player to join the major leagues in baseball's modern era.

WOMEN IN BASEBALL

The ranks of famous baseball players throughout history are full of men. However, some women also had their chance to shine in the sport. By 1942, so many men were fighting in World War II that many minor league teams disbanded. Ballpark owners feared their parks would have to close. In 1943, Chicago Cubs owner Philip K. Wrigley and others founded the All-American Girls Softball League, later changed to the All-American Girls Professional Baseball League (AAGPBL).

There were 60 women chosen for those first female professional teams. Some standouts included Dorothy Kamenshek, who was an infielder and a seven-time All-Star; Dottie Schroeder, a shortstop and powerful hitter who was the only woman to play all 12 seasons the leagues were in action; Doris Sams, a five-time All-Star; and Sophie Kurys, called the "Flint Flash," who stole more than 1,000 bases over her career.

These women's leagues, however, contained all white players. This didn't keep Black women from finding a way to play the sport, however, both before, during, and after the time of the AAGPBL. Three women played alongside men in the all-Black leagues: Toni Stone, Connie Morgan, and Mamie "Peanut" Johnson. Johnson tried to try out for the AAGPBL and was turned away, but she later became the first woman to pitch in an all-Black league, earning a 33–8 record. In 2018, Mo'ne Davis, who became the first girl to earn a win and throw a shutout in Little League World Series history in 2014, helped unveil a mural honoring Johnson and Negro League All-Star Josh Gibson in Washington, D.C.

and Hack Wilson became America's heroes. Baseball came to the radio waves in 1921, allowing those who could not get to a game to catch baseball fever. Attendance at games rose steadily until the Great Depression hit in 1929. Then came World War II (1939-1945), and many players went to war. Baseball continued, however, with players such as Ted Williams, Joe DiMaggio, and Stan Musial making headlines. After the war ended, however, bigger and better changes were yet to come.

ON BASE In college, Jackie Robinson was more well known for playing football than baseball.

A VICTORY FOR EQUALITY

The United States was a very racially segregated country in the years when professional baseball was on the rise. After 1888, Black Americans were not accepted into either the major or minor leagues. In 1920, the Negro National League (NNL) was founded so that Black people could play professional baseball. The Negro American League (NAL) followed in 1937. After World War II, the commissioner of MLB, Happy Chandler, felt that it was wrong to exclude Black men from Major League Baseball when they had fought for their country along with white soldiers. Branch Rickey, then the general manager of the Brooklyn Dodgers, sent scouts all over the country to find a Black player who would be mentally and emotionally strong enough to break the color barrier. They found one playing for the NNL's Kansas City Monarchs—Jackie Robinson.

Rickey asked Robinson if he could tolerate what Black players would hear during games without fighting back. Robinson said he could and was offered a contract to play with the Dodgers. In April 1947, Robinson made his MLB debut. He was named Rookie of the Year. Two years later, he was named the National League MVP.

A GROWING UNDERSTANDING

While these historic and much-needed changes have taken place, the core sport of baseball has not changed much. Still, the way we understand it—and its science—has evolved and grown. While intuition has its place, people understand the mechanics of the game better than ever before. This is also true of the mental and psychological aspect of baseball as well. As we continue to better understand science in many ways, both fans and players will be able to know their favorite game even more, appreciating it for both the intangibles and the core science concepts that make "America's Pastime" what it is today.

CHAPTER TWO

THE PHYSICAL GAME

If asked to name the tools of baseball, the first things that come to mind might be a bat, a ball, a glove, and perhaps a batting helmet. While all these things are important, it's also true that an athlete's body is the most important tool of all. Just like it's important to take care of your sports equipment and keep it in good shape, it's also important to do so with your body. It's actually far more important—after all, you only get one of them!

Even with the best care and intentions, however, accidents happen, both on and off the field. Even minor things can mess with the important piece of equipment that is a peak athlete's body! In 2023, Anthony DeSclafani of the San Francisco Giants had to leave a game because of pain in his left big toe. He'd dropped a piano bench on his foot a few weeks before.

Of course, he's not alone. Other fairly recent and unique injuries have included a hit on the elbow caused by a champagne bottle during a clubhouse celebration, infections caused by recent tattoos, lacerations from animal bites, and various pains caused by errant exercise equipment.

Does it seem odd to you that these seemingless minor injuries could have a game-ending effect on a professional athlete? Remember, baseball (especially at a pro level) is a very physical game that can take a lot of specific, focused activity. A player who can't perform at peak ability can let their team down as well as damage their body further. So, training your body toward peak performance is a very important aspect of science when it comes to sports such as baseball.

BUILDING AND TRAINING

There are many pieces to proper baseball training and conditioning. They focus on developing strength, power, speed, quickness, agility, and flexibility. Proper nutrition is also very important in athletic conditioning. Before the 1980s, strength training was not an important part of conditioning for a baseball player. People viewed baseball as a game of skill and finesse rather than strength, and most managers and coaches saw strength training as something for bodybuilders, not baseball players. They feared that weight lifting and building large muscles would

ON BASE Legendary Hall of Famer Ty Cobb would walk up to 30 miles (48 km) per day with lead in his shoes to keep his lower body strong during the off season.

cause players to become "muscle-bound" and interfere with quickness and proper technique. Today, though, experts better understand the importance of strength training. It's key to playing the game at a high level without injury.

BUILDING MUSCLE

Muscle is a body tissue that's responsible for motion. The human body is composed of three different types of muscles. Cardiac muscle is the muscle of the heart. Smooth muscle makes up the walls of the body's hollow organs, such as the stomach, bladder, and intestines. Skeletal muscles are involved in strength training.

Skeletal muscles are attached to the bones by tough, whitish bands called tendons. Contraction, or shortening, of skeletal muscle is what makes movement possible. A good example of this is the muscles of the upper arm—the biceps on the front and the triceps on the back—which allow a person to bend and straighten the elbow. When a person wants to bend at the elbow, the brain sends a message to the biceps muscle, which contracts and pulls on the tendon to pull the forearm up at the elbow. When the person wants to straighten that arm, the brain sends a message to the triceps on the back of the upper arm. When the triceps muscle contracts, it pulls the forearm down, and the arm straightens. Every such movement of the body depends on the contraction of a muscle.

Skeletal muscles are complex structures. Skeletal muscles, such as the biceps, are made up of thousands of long muscle cells, or fibers, which run the length of the muscle. Groups of muscle fibers work together with a motor neuron, which is a nerve cell that makes the group of fibers contract during movement. The group of fibers along with its motor neuron is called a motor unit.

There are two basic types of muscle fibers. Slow-twitch (ST) fibers contract slowly and do not grow as big, but they do not tire quickly. They are used for movements that require less power and more endurance. Fast-twitch (FT) fibers contract faster and can grow larger, but they also tire sooner. Athletes whose muscles contain more FT fibers excel at sports in which shorter bursts of energy are needed. "There is great variability in the percentage of fiber types among athletes," said exercise physiologist Jason Karp. "For example, it is well-known that endurance athletes have a greater proportion of slow-twitch fibers, while sprinters and jumpers have more fast-twitch fibers."[5] Think about the game of baseball for a minute. Players need to make powerful hits and fast base runs. These are shorter, stronger bursts. That means FT fibers are very important.

Ty Cobb slides into a base during a game in 1924.

ON BASE There are more than 600 skeletal muscles in the human body.

STRENGTH AND POWER

If someone's strong, they have a lot of muscles, right? Not necessarily. Athletes can be quite muscular but lack the corresponding amount of strength, and they can also be strong but lack power. Power is closely related to strength, but power also includes speed of movement. Power means that an athlete can use the maximum amount of strength in the shortest possible period of time. Baseball players must be able to generate explosive power for skills such as hitting the ball hard, pitching a good fastball, and getting from one base to the next as swiftly as possible. The concept of power can be expressed in a formula called the force-velocity relationship:

$$\textbf{Power} = \text{Force} \cdot \frac{\text{Distance}}{\text{Time}}$$

In this equation, "force" is how much strength is applied to move the weight. "Distance" is how far the athlete must move the weight, whether it is a full swing of the bat or the distance between two bases. "Time" is the length of time it takes to move the weight through the distance. Strength training increases the force component of the formula. Power training aims to decrease the time part of the formula, so the athlete can apply strength through the full distance of the movement in the shortest possible time.

To develop explosive power, an athlete's first goal must be to achieve maximum strength for each muscle group being trained. A commonly used statistic is the athlete's 1RM, which stands for "one rep maximum." The 1RM is the most weight a muscle can move in one repetition. Once the athlete has determined the 1RM for a muscle, training focuses on the time part of the force-velocity relationship. Research has shown that moving weight loads that are about 75 to 85 percent of the 1RM is the best way

PAIN AND GAIN

When people lift weights, they place stress on their muscle fibers to move that weight. The stress of moving heavy weights causes microscopic damage to the muscle fibers. Several things happen in response to the damage. First, cells that are part of the immune system release chemicals called cytokines, which cause inflammation and muscle soreness. Second, the body sends increased amounts of fluid and blood to the muscle to help it heal. The damaged fibers also help themselves heal by releasing chemicals that stimulate cell growth. Then, if the athlete allows some time for the muscle to rest, the fibers will become larger and split into new fibers, adding size and strength to the muscle. Allowing the muscle to rest until the soreness is gone is important because without it, the fibers can be torn, the muscle can become weak, and the athlete can become injured.

A muscle also gets larger by recruiting, or activating, new motor units in response to the increased demands of prolonged, intense exercise. During exercise, smaller ST motor units are recruited first, followed by the larger FT motor units. The more intense the workout, the more large, FT motor units are recruited. Over time, the muscle gets larger as more large motor units are recruited.

to shorten the time part of the equation and increase power. For example, a person who can do one squat with 200 pounds (91 kg) of weight might train for power by doing three to five squats with 150 to 170 pounds (68 to 77 kg). Moving weights heavier than 85 percent of the 1RM may build strength but will not develop power as effectively because it limits the athlete's ability to move the weight quickly. This is a part of the equation that's not obvious to many but is very important.

WAYS TO TRAIN FOR POWER

Ballistics is just one method that athletes can use to train for power. This method works by forcing an athlete's muscles to recruit more FT muscle fibers. In ballistics, high amounts of force are applied to low amounts of resistance, or weight, so

Plyometrics can involve explosive jumps up onto a box sometimes called a plyo box.

that the movement is rapid. Unlike traditional weight lifting, in which a majority of the movement is involved with slowing and stopping the movement of the weight, ballistics allows the athlete to move the resistance quickly throughout the entire range of the movement so as not to expend energy to slow and stop the movement. An example of a ballistic exercise is throwing a weighted ball called a medicine ball. The athlete must apply great force to throw the ball but does not expend any energy to stop the movement because the ball leaves their hands at the end of the movement. This increases power in throwing.

Another training method for power is plyometrics. Plyometrics had its beginnings in the training programs of Eastern European athletes in the 1970s. Donald A. Chu, author of *Jumping into Plyometrics*, explained, "As the Eastern bloc countries [countries formerly part of the Soviet Union, such as Romania, Poland, East Germany, and Czechoslovakia] began to produce superior athletes in such sports as track and field, gymnastics, and weightlifting, the mystique of their success began to center on their training methods. Plyometrics rapidly became known to coaches and athletes as exercises or drills aimed at linking strength with speed of movement to produce power."[6]

Plyometrics is similar to ballistics except that in plyometrics, the muscle is put into a lengthening pre-stretch, or eccentric action, before being put into a contracting, or concentric action, as force is applied to the resistance. A muscle that is lengthened just before contracting will contract more forcefully and more quickly, like a spring or a rubber band that is stretched out before being allowed to snap back to its original position.

Plyometric exercises have three phases. Together, the three phases make up the stretch-shortening cycle. The first phase is the eccentric action. In this phase, energy is created and stored in the muscle. Second is the period of time between the eccentric action and the beginning of the contraction. The shorter this time is, the more forceful the contraction will be. The third phase is the actual contraction of the muscle. An example of a plyometric exercise is the squat jump. A person can jump much higher and with more force by crouching into a squat (eccentric action) immediately before jumping upward (concentric action). Athletes can develop power in their legs by doing repetitions of this exercise. This especially applies if the the time between squat and jump is very short.

SPEED AND QUICKNESS

So, strength and power are not quite the same thing. Similarly, neither are pieces of another skill set that's important in baseball: speed and quickness. The goals of speed training are to maximize velocity (how fast the athlete can cover a particular distance), maintain that velocity as the muscles get tired later in the game, and increase acceleration (the change in velocity).

Quickness is related to speed, but it is not the same thing. Quickness refers to how quickly athletes can react to situations and move appropriately, how rapidly they can stop after accelerating, and how well they can suddenly change direction and maintain balance. Quickness measures the speed of adjustment, not how fast the activity is actually completed. Training for speed and quickness is critical in baseball for skills such as running the bases, fielding a sharply hit grounder, and making a tag on a runner.

A DRUG PROBLEM

Drugs have been an unfortunate part of baseball for a long time. Amphetamines designed to give players added energy or focus have been common in major league clubhouses since the 1970s. These drugs were banned by MLB, but they were legal to get from a doctor, so many players either asked their doctor for a prescription or got them from friends with a prescription. Most amphetamines were eventually made illegal by the government; players could no longer get a prescription, but some continued to get them illegally. Today, the only thing amphetamines are legally prescribed for is attention-deficit/hyperactivity disorder (ADHD), and some people suspect athletes of claiming to have this condition in order to get a prescription for Adderall, although these accusations cannot be proven.

Beginning in the 1980s, however, training and conditioning for baseball changed dramatically. Weight training, strict conditioning, and more emphasis on diet resulted in baseball players who were bigger, stronger, and faster than ever before. As superior athletic performance began to translate into multimillion-dollar contracts, players looked for ways to gain a competitive edge and make themselves more valuable. Some players, including some in college and even high school, resorted to taking anabolic steroids—performance-enhancing drugs that increased their body size and strength very rapidly, as well as decreased the time needed to recover from injury.

Anabolic steroids are synthetic, or man-made, forms of the male hormone testosterone. They have been used in medicine since the 1930s to treat abnormal growth as well as illnesses that cause muscle loss, such as cancer and AIDS. When combined with weight training and a certain diet, they can increase muscle mass and strength. With long-term use, however, they can cause abnormally aggressive behavior—often dubbed "'roid rage"—and serious health problems such as high blood pressure, liver damage, and heart disease.

Steroids were banned from use in baseball in 1991, but the ban went largely unheeded and unenforced. In 2002, it was discovered that a company called BALCO had been manufacturing steroids in forms that were undetectable by traditional drug tests. In 2006, Congress began an investigation into the illegal use of steroids by professional baseball players. Its final report named 89 players suspected of having used steroids or other illegal performance-enhancing drugs. In response, MLB instituted tougher measures to prevent illegal drug use by professional baseball players, and many major stars were caught and suspended for using performance-enhancing drugs in the years that followed.

Baseball player Jason Giambi has apologized for using performance-enhancing drugs during his career.

The running that a baseball player does is mostly done in short sprints, rather than over long distances. Training for speed and quickness in baseball focuses on developing quick starts, rapid acceleration, and quick stops. Long periods of slow jogging do little to develop speed and quickness, but sprint training helps athletes shorten their reaction time, reach their top speed quickly, and stop quickly. Running sprints on uphill and downhill slopes increases strength and power in the legs. Short, fast sprints between two cones or bases develop the ability to stop and change direction quickly.

Agility is closely related to and necessary for speed and quickness. Agility is an athlete's ability to move their body, especially their arms, legs, and back, quickly in any direction without injuring the tissues involved in those movements. Agility allows an infielder to dive for a ground ball, get quickly to their feet, and fire the ball to first base, or for a first baseman to scoop a bad throw out of the dirt and still keep one foot on the bag. "When it comes to baseball, speed and agility are important on both sides of the field," said trainer and coach Charles Slavik. "Speed is important in the field where hit balls must be defended. On offense, speed puts pressure on the other team and distracts the pitcher and catcher; this helps the hitter get better pitches to hit. The development of speed and agility is as vital as the development of batting power and throwing arm stability."[7] These skills are also important to avoid injury.

BUILDING FLEXIBILITY

Range of motion is very important to an athlete. This has to do with flexibility, which measures how far an athlete can move a joint without pain. Flexibility is important because muscles, tendons, and ligaments—the tissues that hold the bones together inside the joint—that are too tight restrict joint movement and decrease speed and agility. A lack of flexibility also increases the risk of injuries.

Several factors influence flexibility. The particular structure of each joint determines how far and in what directions it can move. For example, a hinge joint such as a finger or knee can only move up or down, and once it is straight, it cannot move any farther without injury. The wrist can move up and down, side to side, or around in circles. The ball and socket joint of the shoulder has the most movement options of all the joints. Older people tend to be less flexible than younger people, and men tend to be less flexible than women. Very large muscles can inhibit flexibility because their size interferes with the joint's ability to move through its full range of motion (ROM).

The internal environment of the body affects ROM as well. For example, muscles and joints are less flexible when a person first gets out of bed in the morning or when body temperature is low. Previous injuries can also limit flexibility because injured tissues become scarred and thickened, or fibrosed, as they heal. Fibrosed tissues cannot stretch as well as normal, uninjured tissues. Physical therapy can help in some ways but not all.

THE QUESTION OF STRETCHING

Stretching exercises are often considered a very important part of training for agility and flexibility. These allow the muscles and joints to move through their maximum ROM without damage. Many believe stretching is an important part of the warm-up for any exercise program because it helps prevent injury during exercise.

Several different stretching exercises, each with their own purpose in agility and flexibility training, can be used. Static stretching involves slow, constant stretching of a muscle to its maximum stretch and then holding it for 20 to 30 seconds. Static stretching can be active, in which the person provides the force to hold the stretch, or passive, in which a partner or machine provides the force to stretch the muscle. Over time, static stretching increases range of motion of the joints and improves speed and jumping ability.

Many coaches believe static stretching should only be done as a cool-down after exercise is completed rather than as part of the pre-exercise warm-up. They prefer dynamic stretching for the warm-up. Dynamic stretching elongates the muscles using constant movement rather than holding the muscles still. Examples of dynamic stretches are arm circles, walking lunges, and leg swings. Dynamic stretching is also helpful for preventing muscle tightness after exercise.

Ballistic stretching is similar to dynamic stretching, except that ballistic stretching adds a series of bounces to the end of the stretch to increase the range of the stretch. An example is a toe touch with a series of short bounces at the end. Ballistic stretching does help increase range of motion, but it must be done in a careful, controlled fashion. Otherwise, there is a risk of sudden overstretching that can injure the muscle.

Other studies now suggest that stretching before exercise does little to prevent injuries and can even cause further injury during subsequent activity. Still, baseball has a firm tradition rooted in stretching and pregame exercise. Many players still take part in these practices, although some are moving away from them.

NUTRITION

As you see, training is important. However, none of these methods will be effective without proper nutrition. All of the skills needed to play baseball depend on providing enough of the right fuel to the body so the athlete maintains strength, stamina, and mental alertness throughout the game. Nutrients important for baseball players include carbohydrates, proteins, and plenty of fluids, especially water.

A carbohydrate is the fuel the body uses to generate energy for everyday bodily functions, such as breathing and

Many types of fruit contain simple carbohydrates.

digestion, and for fueling muscles during exercise. Baseball players need a fairly high intake of carbohydrates, about 50 to 60 percent of their diet, to maintain their stamina, especially during training periods.

The two main kinds of carbohydrate are simple and complex. Simple carbohydrates are quickly digested and found in foods that have high amounts of sugars, such as candy and other sweets, many fruits, milk, and white bread. The energy they provide tends to last for a short time. Complex carbohydrates take longer to digest. They are found in foods such as whole-grain breads, cereals, and pasta, as well as vegetables. Complex carbohydrates are considered better for a training diet because they are found in foods that have more nutrients and because the energy they provide is more long lasting than that provided by simple carbohydrates.

The second major nutrient important for training is protein. Scientists estimate that more than 50 percent of human body weight is protein. Proteins are everywhere in the body. Lean protein such as that found in poultry, beans, fish, eggs, nuts, low-fat dairy, and lean red meats provides the nutrients necessary for muscles to repair themselves after intense exercise. When protein is digested, it is broken down into smaller "building blocks" called amino acids. The amino acids are then built back into protein and used to build and repair damaged tissues and reinforce muscle fibers, a process called muscle-protein synthesis. Adequate protein intake, combined with proper exercise and rest, helps muscles reach and maintain their condition.

A third component to proper nutrition is adequate intake of fluids during exercise. The body needs fluids, especially water, to carry out its functions and to maintain normal body temperature. Baseball is an outdoor sport, played in spring and summer when temperatures can be high, so the body can lose a significant amount of water, especially from sweating. Sweating also causes the loss of electrolytes, which are essential chemicals that keep the body's systems functioning. This loss can cause problems with people's' stamina, focus, and concentration.

CHAPTER THREE

INJURY AND RECOVERY

Some temporary strains and pulls are common in baseball. However, they're not the only injuries that can happen to a player. Serious injuries in a game have threatened and even ended players' careers. Ligaments can tear, bones can break, and serious head injuries can cause concussions and further trauma. Treatment can be significant, whether it's basic rehab or surgery, and expensive.

Injuries in most sports can have some similarities. They may be considered acute traumatic injuries or overuse injuries, also called cumulative injuries.

CUMULATIVE HARM

Overuse or cumulative injuries are perhaps most common. As the name implies, these are injuries that happen because of repetitive use of a body part over a long time without allowing sufficient time for the body part to heal between episodes of stress. Muscles, ligaments, and tendons can adapt to long-term stress, but if stresses are placed on the tissues too frequently, damage happens faster than rebuilding, so the tissues cannot heal, and they become stiffened with scar tissue and become less flexible.

Overuse injuries can happen for many reasons. They may occur at the beginning of a new workout program if the athlete is overeager and does too much too soon. They may happen to an athlete who does not allow adequate rest time between workouts or to an injured athlete who resumes playing before an injury has fully healed. Overuse injuries can result from poor form, improperly fitted shoes, or inappropriate equipment during workouts or games. Even experienced athletes who have been playing their sports for a long time can get overuse injuries if they increase their training suddenly for some reason. Doing only one kind of exercise over and over again can also lead to an overuse injury.

Diagnosis of an overuse injury can often be made simply by listening to the athlete's description of their symptoms and examining their activity schedule. Symptoms of an overuse injury generally begin with minor pain and stiffness that may interfere with use of the body part. Numbness, tingling, or swelling can also occur if nerves or blood vessels are involved. In some cases, X-rays or other tests may be needed, especially if surgery is being considered as a treatment.

Without adequate treatment, overuse injuries get worse, become more painful, and can prevent the athlete from using the affected part. If not treated properly, they may become unfixable, which can end an athlete's career. Treatment for most overuse injuries starts with the R.I.C.E. method—rest, ice, compression (with an elastic bandage), and elevation. These treatments allow time for recovery and decrease pain and swelling. Pain medications and drugs that decrease inflammation may also be used.

The R.I.C.E. method can help many injuries all on its own, but it is important to always see a doctor for sports injuries.

Many people have to undergo surgical repair of damaged ligaments or tendons.

WEARING DOWN

Overhand throwing is often related to overuse injuries in baseball. These injuries especially affect the shoulder and elbow. "Throwing a baseball is one of the fastest and most violent maneuvers that any joint in the body is subjected to," said Dr. Shane Seroyer, sports medicine physician at the Texas Metroplex Institute for Sports Medicine and Orthopedic Surgery. "The violent and rapid motion places numerous structures in the shoulder at risk for injury."[8]

Pitchers are particularly susceptible to throwing injuries because they may throw more than 100 pitches in a game. For this reason, young pitchers up to the age of 17, whose bones and joints have not stopped growing, are monitored closely to make sure they do not throw pitches that can cause serious damage in the future. According to Seroyer, shoulder injuries from throwing most often come from one of five causes—damaged cartilage, rotator cuff tears, damage to tissues around the shoulder blade, impingement, or neurovascular problems.

The cartilage that surrounds and cushions the shoulder joint is called the labrum. The labrum holds the head of the humerus—the long bone in the upper arm—in place in the socket of the shoulder joint. Tears in the labrum are among the most common shoulder injuries in baseball. As cartilage wears down with age and overuse, tears become more likely. Another common injury occurs to the rotator cuff. The rotator cuff is the name given to a group of muscles and tendons in the shoulder that stabilize it. Overuse of the rotator cuff can cause tears in the muscles and inflammation of the tendons, a condition called tendinitis or pitcher's shoulder. Rotator cuff injuries can cause pain that goes down into the elbow and may weaken the arm (dead-arm syndrome) and decrease throwing velocity. Proper conditioning and throwing technique are very important because treatment of rotator cuff injuries can be difficult.

Pain around the area of the shoulder blade, or scapula, while throwing is most often a result of inadequate conditioning and

ARTHROSCOPIC SURGERY

Arthroscopy is a medical procedure in which the inside of a joint is examined using an arthroscope, a miniature (about pencil-sized) telescope that is inserted into the joint through a small incision about a quarter of an inch long. The surgeon attaches the arthroscope to a camera and a light-carrying cord, which are connected to a video monitor, to see the inside of the joint. The surgeon can also take pictures of the joint with the camera. If the arthroscopy reveals a lot of damage, the joint may be repaired with arthroscopic surgery.

Arthroscopy can be done to evaluate an injury such as torn cartilage or ligaments. The procedure can be used in many joints, including the shoulder, elbow, wrist, knee, ankle, and hip. An advantage of arthroscopy and arthroscopic surgery is that the joint area does not have to be opened up with a large incision. Instead, only two small incisions are made—one for the arthroscope and one for other surgical instruments used for repairing the injury. This reduces pain after surgery, causes less trauma to the surrounding tissue, and decreases recovery time. It also helps reduce scarring so the repaired joint functions better. Athletes who have arthroscopic surgery on their knees, for example, can often be up walking on crutches the next day or even sooner.

Arthroscopy has been around since the 1920s, but it was used mainly to diagnose problems that were then fixed with a larger, more traditional incision. In the 1950s, doctors learned how to use the arthroscope to see what they were doing inside the body during surgery rather than making a larger incision after the arthroscopy had been completed. However, operations were risky because the light bulb in the scope could shatter inside the joint. The development of cold-light fiber optics in the 1970s made arthroscopy safer and more reliable. Today, arthroscopic surgery is one of the most performed orthopedic procedures in the United States.

poor throwing technique, causing the scapula to move in an abnormal way. This kind of injury can also lead to dead-arm syndrome. Impingement is related to scapula pain. This is a term for when the scapula is putting pressure on the rotator cuff. Impingement can cause swelling and pain in front of the shoulder and makes lifting the arm difficult. Neurovascular disorders are another kind of impingement injury caused by overuse. They are more uncommon than other overuse injuries, but they can cause major damage. They happen when nerves or blood vessels are impinged upon by swelling or damaged tissue as they travel through a joint such as the shoulder, elbow, or wrist. The athlete may feel weakness, pain, numbness, or tingling in the arm and hand. Surgery can relieve the pressure on the blood vessel or nerve, and many athletes with this issue will need it.

ELBOW DAMAGE

Overuse injuries are also common to elbows, especially for athletes who are prone to rotator cuff injuries because of improper throwing technique. Frequent, repetitive, hard throwing puts a great deal of strain on the elbow as well as the shoulder. One elbow injury that can be especially damaging is a tear to the ulnar collateral ligament (UCL), a ligament in the elbow. The UCL runs along the inner side of the elbow and, along with the radial collateral ligament (RCL) on the outside of the elbow, stabilizes the elbow and prevents it from moving too much from side to side. Research has shown that the biggest risk factor for UCL damage is the number of pitches thrown, rather than the type of pitches or the style of

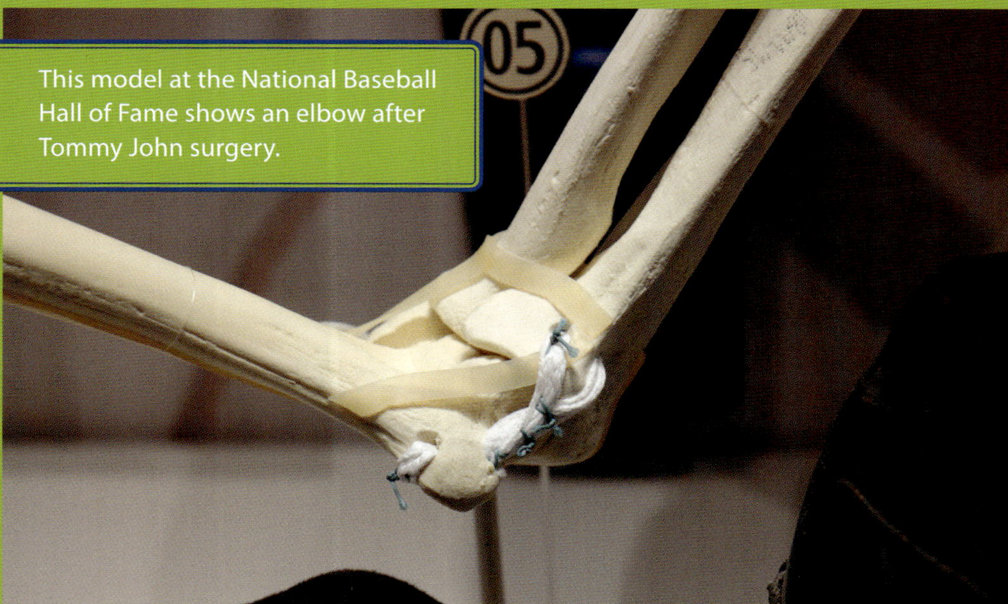

This model at the National Baseball Hall of Fame shows an elbow after Tommy John surgery.

ON BASE Tommy John (Thomas Edward John Jr., born 1943) was nicknamed "The Bionic Man" after his career-saving surgery.

throwing. Throwing breaking balls such as sliders, however, has been shown to increase risk for such injuries.

Until 1974, damage to the UCL meant the end of a pitcher's career. In that year, Tommy John, a pitcher for the Los Angeles Dodgers, became the first professional athlete to undergo surgery to repair his UCL. The procedure became known as "Tommy John surgery." In this procedure, a tendon is taken from the opposite forearm or from below the knee to replace the damaged UCL. As the procedure has improved over the years, the chances for full recovery have reached about 85 to 90 percent. Tommy John returned to the major leagues after his surgery and was able to pitch until he was 46 years old. In 2013, he was the subject of an ESPN *30 for 30 Shorts* documentary.

BROKEN BONES

Overuse injuries develop over time. Acute injuries happen suddenly. This is generally a result of a hard impact or a sudden, abnormal movement of a body part. Some common acute injuries for which baseball players are at risk are fractures, sprains and strains, and torn cartilage or ligaments in the knee.

In October 1914, the *New York Times* reported that "Red Smith, the third baseman of the [Boston Braves], broke his right leg just above the ankle while sliding to second base in the ninth inning of the first game of the double-header. The break was a severe one and it will be a long time before Smith is able to walk. It is doubtful if the Braves' third baseman will ever be able to play ball again."[9] Sliding into a base is the most common cause of bone fractures in baseball. If the cleats catch on the base or in the dirt while the body keeps moving forward, the bones in the lower leg, the tibia and the fibula, can snap near the ankle.

Another cause of broken bones in baseball is being hit by a pitched or batted baseball, especially in an area where

Sliding into base is one of the leading cases of injuries in baseball.

little muscle tissue covers the bone. In July 1967, St. Louis Cardinals pitcher Bob Gibson was hit squarely on the right leg just above the ankle by a hard line drive off the bat of Roberto Clemente. The impact was enough to break the fibula, the smaller of the two lower leg bones.

The chances for full recovery from a broken leg are much better now than they were in 1914, and fractures need not end a player's career. Most leg and ankle fractures are surgically treated with special screws and plates that hold the bones together while they heal. One good thing about bones is that, unlike soft tissues, which form weakened scar tissue as they heal, bones can heal with just as much strength as they had before the fracture. With proper management and enough time allowed for healing, baseball players can come back from most fractures with no loss of ability.

Bob Gibson came back to the Cardinals after two months out and pitched three winning games in the World Series. In March 1997, White Sox third baseman Robin Ventura broke his ankle sliding into home. After he came back in July, he reached base safely in 21 games in a row. More modern examples include Buster Posey, a catcher for the San Francisco Giants, who broke his leg and tore three knee ligaments in May 2011 when Scott Cousins collided with him at home plate. Posey came back at full strength the following season, and by then, the rules regarding blocking home plate had been changed to help prevent that kind of injury from happening again. Players do still break bones sliding, however, including ankle, wrist, and hand bones.

Other common fractures in baseball include fractured fingers and hands from being hit by a pitch or by catching a ball with the bare hand instead of a gloved hand. These are treated with a splint or cast to immobilize the bone and allow it to heal. Bones in the face can be broken from a collision with another player or by being hit with a pitched ball. These fractures may require surgery to line up the broken bones and fix them with tiny metal plates and screws. Less common is "ball thrower's fracture," which refers to a spiral-shaped fracture of the humerus, the bone of the upper arm, caused by extreme muscle contraction and intense torsion, or twisting, from throwing the ball improperly and too forcefully. This fracture is more common in inexperienced and younger players. Doctors treat ball thrower's fractures using a cast and then a brace for a time.

COMMON STRAINS AND SPRAINS

Those who follow baseball know just how common strains and sprains can be in the sport. A sprain is an injury of a ligament. Ligaments support the skeleton and prevent joints from moving in abnormal directions. If the joint is suddenly moved in an abnormal way, the ligament can be overstretched or torn, which makes the joint unstable. Symptoms of a sprain include sharp pain in the joint, swelling, and bruising.

Sprains commonly occur to the knee or ankle, when the athlete steps on an uneven surface (such as a base or another player's foot) and turns the foot or the knee sideways. This overstretches the ligaments along the outer surface of the ankle. Sliding headfirst into a base can cause a wrist sprain. Sprains are classified by their severity as grade 1, 2, or 3. Grades 1 and 2 can usually be treated with the R.I.C.E. method. Prompt treatment can help a sprained joint recover in a few days. If treatment is delayed, recovery can take weeks. Grade 3 sprains can leave the athlete with permanent joint instability, and surgery may be necessary, followed by physical therapy.

A strain is similar to a sprain except that it affects a muscle or a tendon. Strains are caused by overstretching or tearing of the muscle or tendon. They are also classified as grade 1, 2, or 3, depending on severity. Grade 1 strains are commonly called "pulled" muscles. Grade 2 strains involve more tearing of the muscle tissue, but the muscle can still contract. Grade 3 strains involve complete rupture, or a breaking open, of the muscle, and the muscle cannot contract at all. Symptoms of a strain include sudden, sharp pain in the muscle and difficulty using the body part affected. Grade 3 strains, or tears, also include a visible deformity in the torn muscle and bleeding into the muscle.

Lower grade muscle strains are most often treated with pain medicines, such as ibuprofen or acetaminophen, and the R.I.C.E. method, followed by a program of gentle stretching and strengthening. They are generally better after two to three days. More severe strains may require surgery to repair the tear. Athletes may take several weeks (or much longer) to recover.

Baseball players commonly strain a hamstring, the large muscle in the back of the thigh, when they start running suddenly to get out of the batter's box after a hit or to steal a base. Both sprains and strains can be avoided by keeping the muscles and joints flexible, properly warming up before exercise and stretching afterwards, not trying to do too much too soon, and wearing proper footwear for the sport. However, even all this may not be enough.

THE PROBLEM WITH KNEES

Playing sports, including baseball, can be very rough on people's knees. Knee injuries generally involve a tear to the ligaments or cartilage in the knee. Cartilage in the knee is called the meniscus. There are two pieces of this cartilage—the lateral

Ronald Acuña Jr. of the Atlanta Braves has had ACL tears in both legs but recovered.

meniscus on the outside and the medial meniscus on the inside. These C-shaped pieces of cartilage act as cushions between the femur (thighbone) and the tibia (shinbone). A meniscus can get torn when the knee is forcefully rotated or twisted while the foot is planted on the ground. Baseball players can tear their meniscus when making a sharp turn around the bases, by changing direction suddenly in the field, or by colliding with another player.

Symptoms of a torn meniscus include pain, especially when the knee is straightened, and swelling. There may be a clicking or popping sound when the player flexes the knee. A fragment of torn meniscus can get caught between the femur and the tibia and cause the knee to lock. Minor tears can be treated with rest and muscle-strengthening exercises. More severe tears, or minor tears that have become worse over time, may need surgery to remove the torn pieces of cartilage. A period of physical therapy follows surgery until the injury is healed.

The anterior cruciate ligament, or ACL, and the posterior cruciate ligament, the PCL, are the two major ligaments in the knee that hold the femur and the tibia together and stabilize the joint. "Anterior" means front, "posterior" means back, and "cruciate" means shaped like a cross. The ACL crosses in front of the PCL like an "X" so the knee can move forward or backward but not sideways. If the knee is forcefully pushed sideways or twisted, the ACL or PCL can tear. ACL injuries most often happen from sudden changes in direction, abrupt stopping, or landing badly after jumping. The PCL is most commonly injured from a sudden impact to the front of the knee.

Injuries to the cruciate ligaments may not always cause immediate pain, but there may be a loud popping sound as the ligament is torn away from the bone. Treatment depends on the severity of the injury and may range from the R.I.C.E. method, anti-inflammatory pain medications, and physical therapy for partial tears to surgery to repair a completely torn ligament. Some players have had to undergo surgeries in both knees.

INJURY TO YOUNG PLAYERS

While MLB players face injury because of the intensity of major league play, even very young players can be injured. Because children are not fully mature physically, mentally, or emotionally, they are especially prone to certain injuries when playing baseball. Their muscles, tendons, ligaments, and joints are not developed fully, so children are prone to sprains and strains from trying to do too much, especially if they are trying to please their coaches or their parents watching from the stands. Children are less physically coordinated than adults, so they have less control of their bodies. Also, they may not

It is very important for young baseball players to wear equipment that is sized for them.

ON BASE MLB made batting helmets mandatory in 1956.

have a complete understanding of how to move on the playing field, so collisions with other players are common, leading to broken bones and concussions. Young pitchers do not have complete command of their pitches yet, so batters are at risk of getting hit with the ball and suffering bruises, cracked teeth, broken noses, or black eyes. According to the National SAFE KIDS Campaign and the American Academy of Pediatrics, nearly 110,000 children ages 5 to 14 are treated at hospital emergency rooms for baseball- and softball-related injuries each year. These sports also share the highest fatality rate of sports at that age, with three to four children dying from baseball injuries each year, generally due to being hit in the head or chest by a fast-moving ball.

Young pitchers have their own set of injuries that their coaches can help guard against. Pitchers are often pressured to throw more complex, advanced pitches at a young age. Coaches can and should limit the type and number of pitches thrown, depending on the age and skill level of the pitcher. Limiting a pitcher as they develop can prevent early injuries and wear on the arm and elbow later in their career.

Dr. Charles Bush-Joseph, sports medicine specialist at Rush University Hospital in Chicago, said, "For pitchers under fourteen years old, we encourage fastball and change-up [lower velocity] pitches and discourage the use of a curveball to prevent injury."[10] He recommended that pitchers under 10 years old throw no more than 50 pitches per game and 75 per week and that they not throw sliders until they are at least 17 years old. "Breaking" pitches such as curves and sliders require more movement of the arm and place more stress on the shoulder and elbow. Painful overuse injuries such as "pitcher's elbow" (tiny tears in the tendons and ligaments in the elbow) and "little leaguer's shoulder" (which is actually a fracture of the top of the humerus) can result in a player having to miss as much as three months of the baseball season. Some injuries can have lifelong consequences.

CHAPTER FOUR

MOVING PARTS

Baseball is a game of many moving parts. The situations of every baseball game are constantly in flux. Each batter has different skills and tactics, the runners move along the bases, and the score can change incredibly quickly, as can the number of outs. Pitchers are key. They're the only players who touch the ball on every play in a baseball game, because everything starts on the mound. Understanding all the aspects of the game and how to manage them as a pitcher takes years of practice. For one thing, if a pitcher makes a mistake, the pitch may never reach the catcher at all.

Hall of Fame pitcher Warren Spahn once said, "Hitting is timing. Pitching is upsetting timing."[11] Pitchers work hard to get batters out, and most often, they win this battle. This requires a great deal of strategy to go into each pitch. From knowing what type of pitch to throw to actually executing that pitch, working on the mound is never easy. A pitcher has many options when it comes to choosing their pitch, and a good pitcher is skilled at several of them. Each kind of pitch has its purpose and requires its own special delivery from the pitcher.

Pitchers understand the science, especially the physics, behind pitching—the factors that affect how the baseball will travel through the air. Physicist Linda Shore of the San Francisco Exploratorium said, "There's a lot of physics in baseball. When I was a kid, I loved baseball but all I wanted to see was hitting, hitting, hitting. Once I understood the physics of pitching, it became so much more interesting."[12]

Legendary MLB pitcher Sandy Koufax holds up four baseballs representing the four no-hitters he threw.

WINDING UP

The physics of pitching begins with the pitchers themselves. The keys are two basic biomechanical principles: conservation of momentum and sequential summation of movement.

The law of conservation of momentum states that momentum created in a moving object remains the same, or is conserved, even when that momentum is transferred to another object. In physics, "momentum" means how much motion an object has. The amount of momentum a moving object has depends on two things—its mass and its velocity. In mathematical terms, momentum (expressed as "p," thought to come from the Latin word *petere*, meaning "to go forward") is equal to mass (m) times velocity (v), or p = mv.

Mass is not quite the same as weight. Weight depends on gravity; mass does not. Mass is a measure of how much matter an object contains. A bowling ball weighs much less on the moon than it does on Earth because the moon has much less gravitational pull on the bowling ball than Earth does. However, the ball's mass is the same on the moon as it is on Earth; it does

TOOLS OF THE TRADE

There are very specific rules in Major League Baseball about equipment, including baseballs, bats, uniforms, various gloves, and helmets. In many ways, baseballs haven't changed too much over time: They're still made of a core of cork or rubber with yarn wound around it, covered by white leather. A ball can be no larger than 9.25 inches (23.5 cm) around and weigh no less than 5 ounces (142 g), nor more than 5.25 ounces (149 g).

Bats must be one piece of solid wood. They can't be longer than 42 inches (107 cm) long, nor more than 2.61 inches (6.6 cm) across at the thickest part. While the bat handle can be covered or treated to help the player's grip, this is only allowed for a length of 18 inches (46 cm) from the end. Player uniforms must be identical in color and style, with 6-inch (15-cm) numbers on the back. There are a number of rules to make sure they're not distracting in any way.

There are regulations for the catcher's mitt, first baseman's glove, fielding gloves, and the pitcher's glove. There are specific measurements and materials for each of these. Most gloves must be leather, and the measurements can include the depth of the glove and other aspects of its construction. The pitcher's glove cannot be certain specific light shades of color. Catchers must wear a protective helmet and face mask while catching.

not get smaller even though it weighs less. The more mass an object has, the more force it takes to make it change direction or speed when it is moving.

The other force affecting momentum is velocity, or how fast an object is changing its original position. Just as mass is not the same as weight, velocity is not the same as speed. Speed measures how fast an object is moving—how much distance it covers in a certain length of time. Velocity adds direction to speed. For example, a person running on a treadmill may be running at a speed of 8 miles (12.7 m) per hour, but the runner is not moving in any direction, so their velocity is zero.

The second principle, sequential summation of movement, means that if the conserved momentum is transferred from a larger object to a smaller one, it will cause the smaller object to move faster than the larger object that provided the momentum. For example, when a person cracks a whip, momentum builds up in the person's body and is then transferred through the arm, hand, and wrist, then through the whip until it reaches the tip. By that point, the tip is moving so fast that it actually breaks the sound barrier. The "crack" of the whip is a mini sonic boom.

When a pitcher prepares to pitch a baseball, they lean their weight back on one foot and raise their front leg. Momentum builds up in the large muscles of the lower body. As the pitcher moves forward, they lunge their front leg forward and bring their pitching arm back, building more momentum in the lower body and additional momentum in the arm. As they plant their front foot, the lower body stops their forward motion, and the built-up momentum is transferred from the lower body to the torso, which bends forward. As their upper body and throwing arm move forward, the momentum is then transferred from the upper body to the arm, then to the wrist, which snaps like the end of a whip as the hand and fingers finally propel the ball forward. All this momentum, transferred from the large lower body to the much smaller baseball, is expressed in the blistering speed of the ball as it leaves the pitcher's hand. Therefore, although many people think a strong arm is important for a pitcher, a strong lower body is actually more important.

Adding to this is the rotational movement of the pitcher's body around the planted foot. It is similar to a ball being whirled around at the end of a string. The longer the string, the more momentum the ball has and the faster it will move through the air if it is released from the string. This is why taller pitchers tend to be able to throw faster than shorter ones.

One more factor is the height of the pitcher's mound. The standard mound is 10 inches (25.4 cm) high. Because the pitcher steps downhill to release the ball, it adds to the

ON BASE Aroldis Chapman holds the record for the fastest pitch recorded in MLB history. On September 24, 2010, he threw a pitch that was 105.8 miles (107.3 km) per hour!

momentum built into the pitch, thereby adding velocity to the throw.

DELIVERING THE PITCH

Velocity is important. However, it alone does not make a good pitcher. An effective pitcher must be able to fool the batter with a variety of pitches. Since baseball's beginnings, pitchers have invented more than a dozen different kinds of pitches. Each one moves through the air in its own way on its flight to the plate, depending not only on its velocity but also on what spin the pitcher puts on the ball as it is released. Pitchers can vary the way the ball spins by the way they grip the ball and by the way they snap their wrist as they release it. The reason different spins make the ball move in different ways in the air is because of the Magnus force, also called the Magnus effect.

The Magnus effect is named after the German scientist Gustav Magnus, who demonstrated in 1852 that a spinning object will change its path, or trajectory, as it moves through the air, depending on the direction of the spin. As a ball moves

Fernando Valenzuela was a MLB pitcher with a unique style. His nickname was El Toro.

This diagram shows how Bernoulli's principle works.

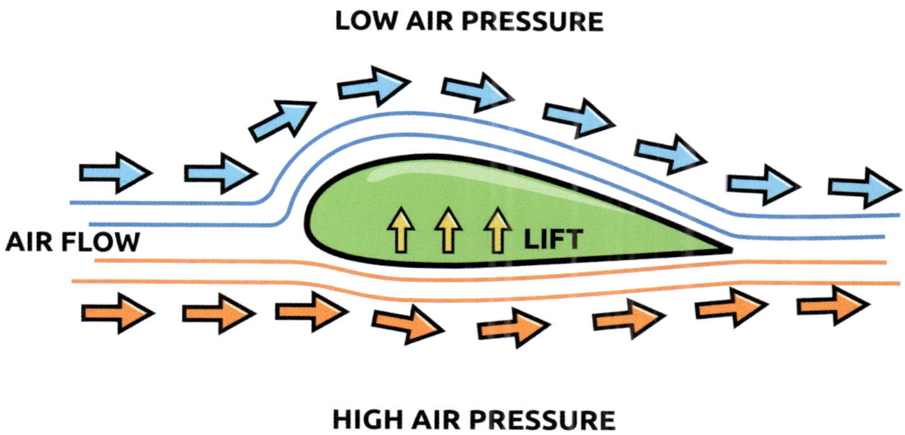

forward through the air, the flow of air is deflected around the ball. If the ball is not spinning at all, the pressure of the air moving around it is equal on all sides, and the ball's trajectory does not change.

When the ball is spinning forward as it moves, the pitcher is said to put topspin on it. When this happens, another principle of physics, Bernoulli's principle, comes into play. First introduced by Swiss mathematician Daniel Bernoulli in the 18th century, Bernoulli's principle says that the faster air moves over the surface of an object, the less pressure the air puts on the object. When a ball has topspin on it, the top of the ball is moving in the opposite direction from the flow of the air (relative to the direction of the ball), but the bottom of the ball is moving in the same direction as the flow of the air. This creates more air resistance, or drag, on the top of the ball and less on the bottom. The drag makes the air move slower over the top of the ball and faster under the bottom. The slower-moving air over the top exerts more pressure on the ball than the faster moving air under the ball. This creates the Magnus effect, which forces the ball to

ON BASE The decrease in velocity of a pitched ball is 1 mile (1.6. km) per hour for every 7 feet (2.13 m) it travels.

move downward as it moves forward. This is how a pitcher throws a curveball.

The opposite happens when backspin is put on the ball. Now the top of the ball is moving in the same direction as the airflow, and the bottom of the ball is moving against the airflow. The increased drag and increased pressure on the bottom of the ball means that the Magnus force makes it stay up rather than sink. A fastball thrown this way may even appear to rise as it approaches the plate.

A pitcher can also put some sidespin on the ball. Sidespin is the kind of spin that a toy top has or, on a larger scale, the kind Earth has as it rotates. A combination of topspin and sidespin makes the ball break slightly to the right or the left as well as down. Most pitchers throw a curveball with a diagonal spin so that it moves both down and to the left of a right-handed batter and down and to the right of a lefty. Right-handed batters tend to do better against left-handed pitchers and vice versa.

GRAVITY: IT'S THE LAW

The force of gravity also acts on a pitched ball. This is the downward pull—created by the mass of Earth—on an object. As a fastball approaches the plate at 95 miles (152.89 km) per hour, gravity causes it to drop as much as 2 feet (0.61 m) from its release point to the plate. A slower pitch, such as a changeup, might drop as much as 5 feet (1.52m), just due to gravity.

The effect of gravity can be seen when a slider is thrown. This pitch has a lateral, or sideways, spin, similar to that of a bullet or a football. Because of this direction of spin, Magnus forces have less effect on a slider as long as it moves in a straight line. When gravity starts to pull it down, however,

BEHIND THE EFFECT

Gustav Magnus was born May 2, 1802, in Berlin, Germany. His father was wealthy, and Gustav (whose first name was actually Heinrich, but he always went by his middle name) was able to attend the best schools in Berlin. After finishing his education there, he went to Stockholm, Sweden, and studied with Jakob Berzelius, a Swedish chemist who, along with several others, is known as a father of modern chemistry. Later, Magnus went to Paris, France, and worked with Joseph Louis Gay-Lussac and Louis Jacques Thénard, both Frenchmen who made important contributions to chemistry and physics. In 1831, Magnus returned to Berlin and became a professor at the university there.

Magnus was very successful and well respected as a professor. He was able to explain complicated concepts clearly and spent a great deal of time with his students, taking them to factories around the city to show them examples of those concepts. He also had students come to his home for discussions about chemistry and physics.

His own research covered a variety of topics, including how gases are absorbed in blood and how heat expands them, the nature of electricity, and the behavior of projectiles fired from guns. This last topic led to his description of the effect of spin on the flight of an object (observations that had actually been made by Isaac Newton almost 200 years earlier), which came to be known as the Magnus effect.

Gustav Magnus died in Berlin in 1870. He spent much of his life as a professor there.

ON BASE Hall of Famer Carl Hubbell is perhaps the most famous MLB player to regularly use the screwball.

the direction of spin changes in relation to the path of the ball. The trajectory of the slider bends, so the ball "breaks" sideways and downward. A slider breaks right to left when thrown by a right-handed pitcher and left to right from a left-handed pitcher. A screwball is like a slider, but it moves the opposite way. However, delivering a screwball is difficult because of the spin necessary to make it break the way it does, so few pitchers throw it. There's also concern that the mechanics of a screwball can lead to injury.

SURFACE MATTERS

Baseballs have stitched seams. This is more important than it might seem, because Magnus forces are even more significant when the ball has a rough surface. There is more drag over the seams than there is over the smooth parts of the ball, so the ball's movement varies depending on how the seams are spinning and how they are interacting with the air. In a two-seam fastball, for example, the pitcher grips the ball with their index and middle fingers lying along two lines of stitches. For a four-seam fastball, the grip is such that their index and middle fingers are lying across the lines of stitches at their widest part. By changing the grip this way, the seams spin differently when the ball is thrown, so the ball behaves differently. Many pitchers believe the four-seam fastball breaks more than the two-seam pitch because of the increased interaction of the seams with the air, creating more of a Magnus effect.

The low-velocity knuckleball has almost no spin at all; it rotates only once on its way to the batter. The slow rotation moves the seams around, which changes the direction of the drag on the ball and allows the ball to be pushed in several directions before it reaches the plate. This makes its motion very unpredictable for the batter as well as for the catcher trying to catch it.

Throughout the history of baseball, pitchers have attempted to trick batters by altering the surface of the baseball to change Magnus forces and make the ball do unpredictable things in flight. They have scuffed the ball with nail files or other objects to increase the drag on one side. In 1987, Minnesota Twins pitcher Joe Niekro was caught with a nail file and a piece of sandpaper that he had used to scuff the ball. In 1980, Seattle Mariners pitcher Rick Honeycutt taped a thumbtack to his finger to cut the surface of the ball. Pitchers have applied substances such as saliva, hair grease, or tobacco juice to the ball to make it slip more easily out of their fingers. Hall of Fame pitcher Gaylord Perry was suspended for coating the ball with so much Vaseline that his catcher could not throw it back to him. Other pitchers have applied substances such as pine tar to make the ball sticky, which they believed would give them a better grip on the ball and create more spin. Altering the surface of a baseball is against the rules and can get a pitcher suspended or fined, but these examples show pitchers' understanding of what surface alterations do to a baseball's spin when thrown.

This photo shows how to hold a knuckleball.

THE NUMBERS BEHIND SPEED

You can calculate the speed of a pitch with this mathematical formula:

Step 1: *Measure the distance from the pitcher's mound to home plate with a measuring tape …*

Step 2: *Time the baseball's pitch from the time that it leaves the pitcher's hand until it reaches the catcher's glove. For example, assume that the baseball's travel time is 0.47 seconds.*

Step 3: *Compute the baseball's average speed in feet per second with the formula S = D/T. The baseball's average speed is "S," the distance that the baseball traveled is "D" and the time of the baseball's travel is "T." If the distance is 60.5 feet and the time is 0.47 seconds, then the speed of the baseball is 60.5/0.47, or 129 feet per second.*

Step 4: *Multiply the speed of the baseball in feet per second by 0.682. This will convert the speed to miles per hour (mph). For example, a speed of 129 feet per second is equal to 129 x 0.682 = 88 mph.*[1]

1. Allan Robinson, "How to Calculate Baseball Pitch Speed," Livestrong, October 20, 2015.www.livestrong.com/article/82686-calculate-baseball-pitch-speed.

MEASURING A PITCH

Even without doctoring the ball, pitchers use their knowledge of science to throw incredibly powerful pitches. These pitches are measured using radar technology.

In 1974, Danny Litwhiler, an outfielder for the Philadelphia Phillies and the inventor of the batting cage, came up with the idea of using a handheld radar gun to measure the speed of pitches. Radar, which started out standing for "radio detection and ranging," was already being used by police to measure the speed of cars to detect people who were driving over the speed limit, and Litwhiler recognized its potential in baseball.

Before radar was invented, many different methods were used to measure pitches. The first test, in 1912, used a machine called a chronograph, which the army used at the time for measuring the speed of bullets. Fans immediately loved knowing how fast their favorite pitchers were throwing. In 1914, the speed of Walter Johnson's pitch was calculated by having a motorcycle drive away from Johnson at a constant speed. Experts measured the distance between the pitcher and the motorcycle when the pitch was thrown and when the ball hit the target to calculate the speed of the pitch. Over time, new types of chronographs were used as technology improved, but radar is currently used because it gives the most accurate measurement.

Radar guns work by shooting radio waves at a baseball and measuring the frequency of the waves the baseball makes as it travels through the air. This frequency changes as the ball moves. *Hardball Times* explained:

> *If the ball is at rest, the waves reflect off it at the same frequency as they arrive … When the ball comes toward the radar gun … the waves it sends back to the gun have a higher frequency. The radar detector inside the gun sends the change in frequency to an internal computer that calculates and displays the speed of the ball.*[13]

Some people believe the radar detector adds 5 miles (8 km) per hour to a baseball's speed, but even if this is true, some MLB pitchers' ability to throw a 100-mile (161 km) per hour pitch is impressive. According to the *Huffington Post*, "once that speed is reached additional mass does not help you throw the ball any faster. It has been calculated that there are around 80 newton-meters of torque [rotational force] acting on the elbow of the pitcher throwing a ball at 100 [miles per hour]. If any more torque is placed on the elbow it would likely snap."[14]

CHAPTER FIVE
HARD HITTING

Talented baseball players make hitting a baseball look easy, but it's not! If fact, even the best hitters in the history of baseball barely managed to get more than 3 hits for every 10 at bats.

Hitting a ball thrown by a pitcher involves different body systems; a player uses reflexes, sight, and many muscles. Good body mechanics, power, and endless practice have made batters more prepared than ever. Some say the most difficult skill in all of sports is to hit a round ball with a round bat, and it is made even more complicated by the skill of the pitcher. A batter standing at home plate has about one-quarter of a second to make a judgment about the speed and direction of a ball that is 3 inches (7.6 cm) wide and hurtling at 90 miles (144.8 km) per hour from the pitcher's mound only 60 feet 6 inches (18.2 m 15.2 cm) away. Then, batters still have to make the decision about whether or not to swing at the ball and, if they decide to swing, where and when to swing the bat to make good contact with the ball. Even after good contact is made, that's just the beginning.

EYES ON THE BALL

People learning to play baseball may be told, "Keep your eye on the ball." That advice works fine at lower levels of play when the ball is coming toward the plate at a relatively slow velocity. At the major league level, however, that advice is of little help because the human eye is not capable of remaining

ON BASE Legendary Red Sox hitter Ted Williams's vision was so good he could read the label on a record turning at 78 revolutions per minute—far beyond most people's ability.

focused on a baseball moving at 90 miles (144.8 km) per hour. Ken Fuld, professor of psychology at the University of New Hampshire, said it is physically impossible for a hitter to keep their eye on the ball all the way to the plate. "Good hitters fixate on a pitcher's release point," he explained, "and then make an eye movement (called an eye saccade) to track the ball (called a smooth pursuit eye movement) for as long as possible. A good hitter can track the ball to within about 5 feet (1.5 m); a not-so-good hitter loses eye contact at about ten feet."[15]

According to Yale University professor Dr. Robert Adair, author of *The Physics of Baseball*, once the ball leaves the pitcher's hand, it takes about a 10th of a second (0.1 second) for the batter's eye to see the ball and send the information to the brain. The brain needs another 0.075 second to process this information and decide the location and velocity of the pitch. In that time, 0.175 second (less than one-fifth of a second), the ball has already traveled 14 feet of its 60 feet 6 inches (4.3 of its 18.4 m) to the plate. The batter now has about 0.125 second to decide when and where to swing. By then, the ball is only

Ted Williams was one of the greatest hitters in the history of baseball. He had great vision and a powerful swing.

25 feet (7.6 m) away. The swing itself lasts about 0.15 second, and at that point, the ball has arrived. A batter who decides at the last instant not to swing must react within the first 0.05 second of the swing to pull the bat back. It is not fully understood how a human being can predict where a fast-moving ball will be when it arrives, but some clues help the batter "see" the pitch and know what to expect from it.

First is the angle of the pitcher's arm as the pitch is delivered. An overhand delivery may indicate a pitch with more backspin, whereas a more sidearm delivery might indicate sidespin on the ball. Another clue is how soon or late in the delivery the pitcher releases the ball and at what angle the ball is leaving their hand. For example, a fastball is released with a slightly downward angle, whereas a slow changeup is delivered with a slightly more upward angle before gravity pulls it down on its way to the plate.

Another clue is how the pitcher is holding the ball. Different grips are used to produce different pitches, and a good batter can see the grip and judge the pitch as it is released. Another effective skill for a batter to have is the ability to judge what spin the ball has on it as it approaches. Depending on the spin, the red seams on the white ball create different images as the ball rotates because of the way the seams pass in front of the batter's view. For example, a four-seam slider appears to the batter to have a red dot on the upper right part of the ball as it spins, but a two-seam slider appears to be solid white at the top. This skill of seeing a pitch and reacting to it requires excellent dynamic visual acuity—the ability to see and interpret moving objects. Even with years of practice, even the best batters will still miss.

IN THE SWING OF THINGS

The body mechanics of hitting involve how the batter uses their body to generate maximum force on the ball. The batter stands at the plate with knees bent and hands back, like a tightly coiled spring, ready to swing. As the batter swings, they bring the bat around and turn their upper body, using

THE PROBLEM OF CORKED BATS

Just as pitchers have been known to alter the surface of the ball to give them an advantage, batters have also been known to alter the bat in an effort to give them an edge. One way they have done this is by using a "corked" bat. A corked bat is a bat that has been hollowed out and filled with another substance such as cork or small rubber balls. The hole is generally about 1 inch (2.5 cm) in diameter and about 10 inches (25.4 cm) long.

MLB player Sammy Sosa was suspended for seven games in 2003 after using a corked bat. Sosa said he used the bat by accident, and the rest of his bats were clean.

The results of a corked bat and its advantages and disadvantages are not fully known. A corked bat might help a batter because it is lighter. Also, because the lighter material is out near the barrel end of the bat, the balance point of the bat is shifted closer to the batter's hands. Both of these changes help the batter get a faster bat speed during their swing, which allows more time to react to the pitch and make a decision about swinging. The lighter weight also gives more control over the swing.

One possible disadvantage to using a corked bat is that the part of the bat that makes contact with the ball has less mass than a solid wood bat. This cancels out some of the advantage of the faster bat speed. Additionally, corked bats have not been proven to increase the chances of hitting a home run. In fact, research has demonstrated that there is little or no real advantage to using a corked bat. Another consideration is that, like altering the ball, corking the bat is against the rules, and batters who are caught will be suspended or fined.

Isaac Newton's laws of motion have a lot of impact on baseball and other sports.

rotation to add energy just as the pitcher does. The batter may take a step forward to shift their weight forward and add some momentum to the swing, but they keep their back foot planted firmly on the ground so all the energy generated in the swing stays in the upper body and arms. The momentum built up in the batter's body is transferred to the smaller bat, which generates a fast bat speed and a lot of kinetic energy.

Kinetic energy is the energy created by a moving object. When an object with kinetic energy in it hits another object, the kinetic energy is transferred to the hit object, which makes it move. The faster the object is moving, the more kinetic energy it has and the faster the hit object will move when it is hit. An object with more mass also imparts more energy than a lighter one.

NEWTON AND BASEBALL

Multiple laws of nature were observed in the 17th century by English scientist Isaac Newton. Newton, among many other accomplishments, devised the three laws of motion. The second and third of these laws are the most relevant to baseball. Newton's third law of motion says that for every action, there is an opposite and equal reaction. This means an object that is pushed against pushes back with an equal force but in the opposite direction.

SIR ISAAC'S LAWS

Isaac Newton (1643–1727) was a renowned mathematician and scientist who, while still in college, developed theories about the physics of motion, light, and gravity. For his work, he was knighted by Queen Anne in 1705. His three laws of motion are listed below.

One: An object at rest tends to stay at rest, and an object in motion tends to stay in motion at the same speed and in the same direction, unless acted upon by an unbalanced force. If someone pushes on both sides of a ball, the ball does not move because the force is balanced. If they push on just one side, the ball will roll because the force is unbalanced. Another example is that passengers in a car continue to move forward when the car stops suddenly, until stopped by their seatbelt.

Two: The greater the mass of an object, the greater the force needed to move the object. This can be expressed in the mathematical equation force equals mass times acceleration, or $F = ma$. Although weight and mass do not refer to the same measurement, they are about equal on Earth, so the object's weight can be used for mass in this calculation. If someone knows the weight (mass) of an object and how fast it is moving (acceleration), they can figure out how much force is being applied to it. Force is measured in units called newtons.

Three: For every action, there is an opposite and equal reaction. This means that when an object pushes another object, the first object pushes back in the opposite direction with equal force. For example, when a fish pushes water backward with its fins, the water pushes the fish forward with equal force, which makes it possible for the fish to swim.

In baseball, both the ball and the bat exert force on each other when they make contact. The reason the bat moves the ball but the ball does not move the bat has to do with Newton's second law of motion, which says that the object with the greater mass or greater speed puts more force on the object with less mass or less speed. Newton's second law can be expressed in an equation similar to the one used to express conservation of

ON BASE Every regulation baseball has exactly 108 raised, red stitches.

momentum: Force (F) is equal to mass (m) times acceleration (a), or F = ma.

Bat speed and pitch speed are often close to equal in acceleration, so since the mass of the bat is greater than the mass of the ball, more force is put on the ball than on the bat, and the ball is sent flying. A batter can also send a ball farther by using a larger bat (with more mass), as long as the batter has enough power to maintain the same bat speed.

A fast swing and a heavy bat are only part of hitting a ball far, however, because the ball is also moving at a high velocity. The kinetic energy transferred from the bat to the ball provides some of the energy that sends the ball flying, but not all of it. There is also kinetic energy in the ball. When both objects involved in a collision are moving instead of just one, the resulting reaction is greater. This is why a bunted ball does not go very far; the bat moves very little—if at all—on a bunt attempt.

In addition, a fast swing, along with a fast pitch, creates more kinetic energy than it would with a slower pitch. The ball will fly off the bat faster. And the faster it flies, the farther it will go.

BOUNCING BACK

Elasticity is another baseball physics factor. When two objects collide, the surface of both objects is dented or compressed to some degree, as long as the objects are not absolutely rigid. The faster the object resumes its original shape, the more elasticity it has. For example, if a person pushes their finger against an inflated balloon, the balloon bounces back to its original shape as soon as the finger is removed. Balloons have a lot of elasticity. If the person presses their finger into a ball of clay, the hole it makes stays there. The clay does not return to its original shape because clay has almost no elasticity.

ON BASE Swinging the bat even 1/100 of a second too soon or too late will cause the ball to go foul. Swinging too soon or too late can also cause the batter to miss the pitch altogether.

Even though a bat is made of wood or metal and a baseball seems to be very hard, both of them have some elasticity. Ultra-slow motion photography shows that when the bat makes contact with the ball, both surfaces are compressed to some degree, but they both spring back to their original shape within a few thousandths of a second. During the collision, some of the kinetic energy is converted into heat, caused by the friction of the two surfaces contacting each other. The faster the ball and bat bounce back to their original shape, however, the less kinetic energy is lost as heat, and the more energy is conserved as motion. Elasticity helps to conserve kinetic energy. This is sometimes called the trampoline effect. When a person jumps on a trampoline, most of the kinetic energy of the jump is conserved because the trampoline is elastic and resumes its shape quickly, propelling the person into the air. This trampoline effect is even greater if both objects (such as a ball and bat) have elasticity.

SPIN DOCTORS

You've read that the effect of spin can be important in pitching. The effect of spin on a baseball is just as important in hitting. Spin is a major factor in determining how far a ball will travel after it is hit. Imagine a bat hitting a ball in slow motion. If the bat contacts the ball on its upper half, it will make the ball spin forward. In other words, it will have topspin on it. Just as a pitched ball with topspin tends to drop because of the Magnus effect, a ball hit with topspin will also tend to drop, which generally results in a ground ball that hits the ground in front of the fielders.

Conversely, if the batter hits the ball on its lower half, the ball will have backspin. Magnus forces will cause the ball with backspin to stay up longer, so it will go farther. Home run hitters not

HISTORY OF HOMERS

Very little can enliven a ballpark (or a baseball diamond of any sort) like a home run. Home runs are scored when a batter hits the ball in way that allows them to round all the bases and make it back to home plate in one play with no errors. This usually involves the ball being hit over the outfield fence and never touching the ground, but inside-the-park home runs can happen too.

Ross Barnes of the Chicago White Stockings hit the first major-league home run in 1876. The chase for home runs didn't really get going until the "live ball" era started in 1920. (In fact, players were sometimes discouraged from trying to hit them, because they'd often just hit fly balls that were promptly caught.) Babe Ruth joined the Yankees that year and hit 54 home runs. Baseball's love affair with home runs had begun.

Barry Bonds holds the record for most MLB home runs with 762, although this accomplishment (in 2007) has been tainted by his alleged connection to performance-enhancing drugs. Only eight other players have hit more than 600 home runs, led by Hank Aaron with 755, Babe Ruth with 714, and Albert Pujols with 703. Josh Gibson of the Negro Leagues may have hit more home runs than even Bonds, perhaps as many as 950. However, the poor record keeping for the leagues hasn't allowed historians to verify this.

Babe Ruth hit what's considered MLB's longest home run (575 feet [175 m]) in 1921. The longest home run verified by modern technology was 505 feet (154 m) in 2019, hit by Nomar Mazara.

only have power, they also know how to hit a ball with enough backspin to keep it up long enough to carry it right out of the park for a home run. The more a batter "gets under" a ball, however, the more backspin it will have, and the more vertical its trajectory, or flight path, will be. Too much backspin results in a pop fly. Gravity will bring it down to the fielder before it reaches the fence. If the batter really gets under the ball, the ball will go straight up.

If a batter hits the ball squarely in the center, little spin will be put on it. This results in a line drive. A skilled batter can hit a hard line drive with enough topspin to make it land in front of the outfielder for a base hit, or enough backspin to make it go past the outfielder. Pitchers often throw certain pitches to make hitters put balls where pitchers want them to go. A fly ball pitcher wants batters to get under the ball for fly outs, while a ground ball pitcher wants batters to top pitches and ground out to infielders. Changing things up makes it even harder for hitters.

AIR RESISTANCE

Understanding physics can help baseball players in many ways. Good hitters use spin and its effect on air resistance to get a good hit. Air resistance also greatly affects the flight of a ball after it is hit. When a baseball is first hit, the momentum transferred to it and the Magnus forces acting on it are enough to overcome the pull of gravity for a short time. Soon, however, air resistance comes into play to slow the ball down.

Whenever two objects rub against each other, friction is created. Friction changes kinetic energy into thermal energy, or heat, so some kinetic energy is lost. For example, people who feel cold might rub their arms to use friction to warm them. A baseball traveling through the air collides with the molecules of air, causing friction between the air molecules and the ball. Some of the ball's kinetic energy is lost as thermal energy because of the friction.

At higher altitudes, air is thinner. It has less density, which means the air molecules are farther apart than they are at lower altitudes, so there is less friction between the ball and the air. Professional ballplayers know that it is often easier to hit a home run in Denver, Colorado, than in New York or Florida because the air density in the mountains 1 mile (1.6 km) above sea level is much lower than it is at sea level. When the velocity of the ball has decreased enough because of air resistance, gravity takes over, and the ball heads down toward the ground.

Air interferes with the flight of the ball in several other ways, depending on wind speed and direction, air temperature, and humidity. Wind alters the effect of friction on the ball. If the wind is blowing in the same direction as the ball, less friction is created, and the ball will carry farther than it would have if the air were still. However, if the wind is blowing against the ball, it causes more friction and increases the resistance; thus, a ball that might have been a home run now becomes a long fly ball. Good batters know how to take advantage of wind speed and direction.

As former MLB catcher Brian Johnson said, "Sometimes the wind might be blowing somewhat in towards the plate in left field, and slightly out of the park in right [field]. In that case, [the batter] might take advantage by trying to hit the ball towards right."[16] Candlestick Park in San Francisco, California, Johnson's former home field, was known for its "jet stream" wind that often blows in from left field toward right field. Batters who sent the ball toward right field could take advantage of that current to send the ball out of the park. Each park in the major leagues has different qualities that affect the ball; the height of the stands, its proximity to bodies of water, and the direction the park is facing all factor into the physics of the baseball's movement.

Besides air density and wind speed, the temperature and humidity of the air can affect the flight of the ball. When air is warm, it expands, which means the air molecules become farther apart. Warm air is less dense and exerts less pressure and friction on the ball, so the ball tends to travel farther in warm air than in cooler air. Humid air, which has a lot of water vapor in it, is also less dense than dry air when they are the same temperature. This is because molecules of water vapor weigh less than molecules of oxygen and nitrogen, the two most common components of air. The more water molecules are in the air, the less dense it is, and the less friction it puts on the baseball. This is all important to the sport.

CHAPTER SIX

TEAM EFFORT

Hitting and pitching are important parts of baseball. However, when the batter does manage to put a ball in play, the other eight players on the field are there to help the pitcher get an out. Fielding percentages are higher than batting averages because baseball players have plenty of tools at their disposal to get batters out.

Baseball doesn't have an overall time clock. The main timekeeper is an out. Three outs end an inning. There is plenty of science at play in catching fly balls and throwing the ball to get runners out. Just as in pitching and hitting, science, especially physics, is involved with the skills of catching the ball. Well-developed skills involving the eyes, brain, and muscles are necessary to catch (and throw) the baseball successfully.

CAUGHT!

Several factors determine where the ball will go once it is hit and how fast it will get there. The speed and location of the pitch, the swing of the bat, the spin on the ball, the temperature of the air, and the air resistance all affect the ball's trajectory. Fielders must know how to make rapid judgments about how the ball comes off the bat and where the ball is going, and they must react quickly to those judgments.

Fielders have to know how to handle balls hit on the ground and into the air. Ground balls behave differently than balls hit into the air because different forces act on them. A quick reaction time is needed by a fielder to get in front of the ball before it gets by them. The goal is to get it in the glove, transfer it to

GLOVES THROUGH THE YEARS

Can you imagine the force of a baseball hitting your bare hands? In the early days of baseball, players wore no gloves at all. Once batters began hitting the ball harder, however, more players decided to wear protection for their hands. The first gloves looked more like today's batting gloves than fielder's gloves. The fingers were uncovered, and the palm of the glove had only a little padding. Some players made their gloves from old mittens, which is where the word "mitt" comes from. By the end of the 1870s, most players wore gloves. The first specialized mitt was a catcher's mitt created by New York Giants catcher Buck Ewing in the 1880s.

The price of a baseball glove can run from inexpensive to astronomical!

Early gloves were made of horsehide, cowhide, or buckskin. One of the most important improvements was made in 1920, when webbing was added to the space between the thumb and first finger to form a pocket for catching the ball. Since then, glove manufacturers have created different styles of webbing. Pitchers like a closed web because it helps them conceal their grip on the ball from the batter. Some infielders, such as former Cardinals shortstop Ozzie Smith, like the "sixth finger" web style, in which the webbing looks like it has a sixth finger sewn into it between the thumb and index finger.

Today, gloves are specialized for different positions. Outfielders use large gloves with long fingers for maximum reach on fly balls. Infielders use smaller gloves so they can get the ball out of the glove faster. First basemen and catchers use mitts designed without individual fingers for catching fastballs or for scooping bad throws out of the dirt. Catchers may also wear special, larger gloves when catching so they have a better chance of catching tougher-to-follow pitches.

the throwing hand, and throw it quickly to the right place to get the out. Infielders ready themselves by standing with their knees slightly bent and their weight shifted forward as the pitch is made. This allows them to move quickly in any direction in response to a hit coming their way. If there is time, the fielder will "round the ball," which means taking a few steps toward the ball and then moving slightly to the right (for a right-handed thrower) so the ball is fielded near the left foot. With their weight already on the left foot, fielders can then take a step or a short hop toward first base on the right foot, and their momentum will carry them forward toward first base, which helps them throw smoothly and quickly.

Since baseballs have a certain amount of elasticity, they bounce when they hit the ground. It can be a challenge for a fielder to "read" the bounce to know where the ball will be when it gets to them and where to position their glove to make a clean catch. Balls bounce differently on the dirt of the infield than they do on the grass. Dirt is harder than grass, so when the ball hits, its surface is compressed more than it is on grass. The ball's elasticity then causes it to rebound, or bounce, more than it does on the softer grass surface. Also, grass, because of its thickness and rough texture, puts more friction on a rolling ball than dirt does. The added resistance slows the ball down. Fielders know this, so they move toward the ball faster if it is rolling on grass than if it is rolling on dirt. Still, it can be

Catchers often have different gloves than players in other positions.

impossible to know for sure where a ball will bounce. A player's expectations come from endless practice and experience on various surfaces, but there are always "bad" or unexpected bounces that can happen for a variety of reasons. There's a lot of unpredictability in the game still.

IN AN ARC

Nearly any kind of hit can be unpredictable, but a ball hit in the air can come at the fielder in an almost infinite number of ways. A hard line drive will travel in a flat, straight trajectory and can get to an infielder in less than a second. A pop-up may go almost straight up off the bat. Most balls hit in the air, however, travel upward for a while before gravity pulls them back down. The fielder must judge both the speed and the trajectory of the ball to be at the point where the ball is within reach in time to catch it before it hits the ground.

The trajectory of a fly ball is curved somewhat like the arc of a rainbow, but the shape of the curve is a little different. While the curve of a rainbow is a half circle, the trajectory of a fly ball follows a path called a parabola. A parabola is a curve used in advanced mathematics, but examples of it can be seen in everyday situations. Besides a fly ball, other examples of a parabola are the path formed by the stream of water coming out of a drinking fountain and the arc of the St. Louis Gateway Arch.

One exception to the parabolic path is the pop-up that goes vertically up behind home plate. This hit goes almost straight up because of the huge amount of backspin put on it from the batter hitting the ball hard but undercutting it. This kind of hit is especially difficult to catch because, unlike other fly balls, it does not follow the typical parabolic trajectory, nor does it go straight up, then straight back down again. Because of the excessive backspin, the Magnus force on these hits creates a trajectory that is, at first, curved backward toward the backstop in a very steep path upward, until the ball reaches the peak of its trajectory. At that point, gravity takes over, and the Magnus force reverses direction and actually causes the ball to loop back on itself and cross its own upward path on its way back down, like a stunt flier doing a loop-the-loop. Inexperienced fielders who believe they have positioned themselves properly underneath such a ball may find themselves completely fooled when the ball actually curves away from them as it approaches the ground. Physics is predictable, but it may not always be so in an obvious way to the observer!

PREDICTING THE PATH

Even if they don't think they understand the physics of baseball, good fielders learn to predict the path of a fly ball. A good deal of research has been done on how a fielder learns this. Yale physicist Dr. Robert Adair believes that one important clue for the fielder is the sound that is produced as the bat contacts the ball. "Sometimes the difference between the sharp acoustic crack-of-the-bat [acoustics is the science of sound] and a sullen acoustic clunk-of-the-bat can be worth a run or two,"[17] he said. If the hitter connects solidly with the ball, a "crack" sound is caused by air being suddenly forced out between the ball and the bat.

"If you don't hit the ball squarely you hear the bat vibrate," Adair said. "That produces a thudlike sound that gives an experienced player a clue that the ball hasn't been hit too well."[18] He said that sound reaches the fielder 1.7 seconds before visual cues indicate the flight of the ball. In that short period of time, the fielder can run about 50 feet (15.2 m), an important advantage in getting to the ball on time.

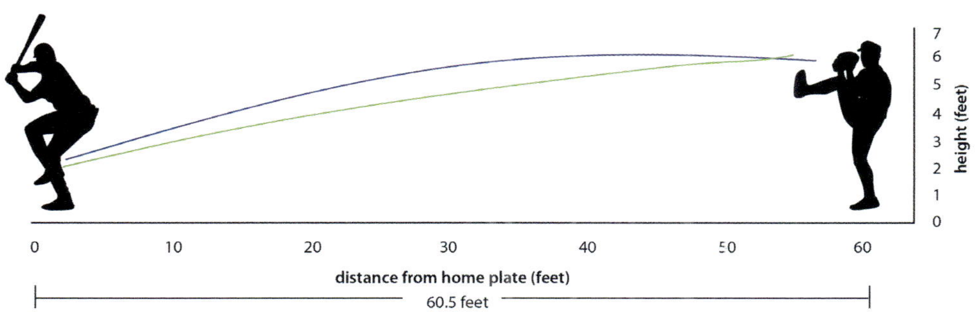

Pitches also have trajectories, as shown here.

ON BASE When hitting a thrown ball, bats vibrate at different frequencies.

Former Baltimore Orioles outfielder Melvin Mora agreed. If he heard the crack, he would run farther out; a clunk, and he moved closer in. "As soon as I hear the sound of the bat, I know where the ball is going," he said. "It's about reaction. It's something I can't explain."[19]

The task for the outfielder is to judge two things: the steepness of the angle at which the ball is rising and the velocity of the ball. This information gives the fielder some idea of how far the ball will go. A ball that comes off the bat at a steep angle will go higher into the air than a ball that comes off the bat at a lower angle. If both hits have the same velocity and if there is little resistance from the wind, the higher hit ball will not travel quite as far as the ball with lower trajectory because more of its kinetic energy is used to go up rather than out and away from the plate. This tells the fielder whether to move in or out. A ball pitched and hit with more velocity will travel farther because it has more kinetic energy overcoming gravity than the ball with less velocity. This gives fielders some indication of how much time they have to get to the ball.

It is more difficult for fielders to judge balls that are hit right toward them than balls that are hit to their right or left. This is because there is less visual information coming to the fielders. If the ball is hit right at them, they can see it go up, but they cannot as accurately judge the steepness of the angle at which it comes off the bat. It is also harder to judge the velocity of the ball if it is coming straight toward them. They know that they do not have to move right or left to catch the ball, but it is more difficult to judge how far in or out they must move to meet the ball. If a ball is hit right or left, fielders can judge the velocity and the angle at which it is rising, and this gives them important visual information for judging where the ball will come down.

A THEORY OF OPTICS

So, it's more difficult to catch fly balls. Still, fielders manage to catch fly balls hit directly at them more often than not. Physicist Seville Chapman devised a theory to explain how fielders catch this kind of hit. He called the theory Optical Acceleration Cancellation, or OAC. He theorized that as fielders move their position forward or backward, the rate at which the ball moves through their field of vision speeds up or slows down. If fielders move closer to the ball, it passes through their field of vision faster. If they move too far forward, they will soon realize that the ball is rising too quickly to adjust position, and the ball will sail over their head. If they move backward, the ball travels through their field of vision more slowly, but if they move too far back, they will not be able to adjust their position in time to keep the ball from landing on the ground in front of them.

Rather than run to where they think the ball will land and then stand there and wait for it, good fielders constantly make forward or backward adjustments to their positions so the ball maintains a constant speed as it moves through their visual field. University of Missouri

MLB players work with physics during every play!

ON BASE A grand slam is when there are base runners at first, second, and third bases when a batter hits a home run.

psychologist Dr. Mike Stadler, author of *The Psychology of Baseball*, explained:

> *By "controlling" the way the ball moves across the image [field of vision], the player can guarantee that he will arrive at the place where the ball will land at the same time as the ball. This strategy is called an "error nulling" strategy because the player's movement is determined by the ball. If the ball strays from its trajectory (say, because of wind resistance), then the fielder will have to change his movement in sync with the changes in the ball's movement to keep it progressing in the same way through his field of view. So the system is assumed to employ a feedback loop: Monitor the optical acceleration. If it is increasing, slow down. If it is decreasing, speed up. Repeat.*[20]

ANOTHER THEORY

Of course, not every hit ball is the same. If the ball is hit to the right or the left of the fielder, rather than directly at them, the player can see the actual arc of the ball's rise and see how fast it is moving. This added visual information increases the chances that the fielder will get to the ball in time to catch it. Building on the earlier work involving OAC, psychologist Michael McBeath developed another theory of catching fly balls called Linear Optical Trajectory, or LOT. LOT is similar to OAC in that the fielder still uses the path of the ball through their line of vision to make adjustments to their own path of movement, but it adds the side-to-side dimension as well as the vertical dimension.

Both OAC and LOT describe what information the eyes perceive and send to the brain for processing. How that information is processed in the brain and how it leads to a physical response is not known for sure, but two theories are debated

MAYS AND "THE CATCH"

Throughout the history of baseball, countless memorable defensive plays have been made by outfielders, but one particular play might be the best known among baseball fans. It is simply known as "The Catch."

It was the top of the eighth inning in Game One of the 1954 World Series between the New York Giants and the Cleveland Indians. With two runners on base, Cleveland's Vic Wertz came to the plate. On the fourth pitch, he connected solidly and sent the ball far into deep center field. Giants center fielder Willie Mays had been playing shallow, and when he saw how the ball was flying, he turned and ran hard straight toward the center field wall. At the warning track, and without turning around, he caught the ball over his shoulder, looking more like a football player catching a long pass. Larry Doby, the runner on second, had taken off as soon as the ball was hit, never dreaming that it would be caught. Mays spun around and fired the ball back to second base, his momentum causing him to fall to the ground, and doubled off Doby, who had already rounded third on his way to home.

Mays himself said later that he did not consider "The Catch" to be his best defensive play. It may be as memorable as it is because it was a World Series game or because it was one of the first games broadcast on television in the very early days of TV.

In 2006, University of Illinois at Urbana-Champaign physicist Dr. Alan Nathan reported that if the air temperature had been one degree warmer that day, "The Catch" would never have happened. Because of the lower resistance of warmer air, the ball would have traveled 2 more inches (5 cm)—just out of the reach of Mays's glove.

among scientists: Information Processing (IP) and Ecological Psychology (EP).

TWO THEORIES

The IP theory of human perception and processing compares the human brain to a computer. Its past experiences are considered a memory bank. The senses send input from all life experiences to the brain, where information is stored in a memory system. The brain also has a "main processor" that takes new input and combines it with data already in memory to solve new problems as they arise. This is how people know, for example, that if their senses tell the brain that they are cold, they have several alternatives to solve the problem, including putting on a coat, turning up the heat, or having a warm drink.

Applied to catching a fly ball, IP theory suggests that the fielder's sense of sight sends information about the flight of the ball to the brain, where the information is combined with previously stored data about all the fly balls caught in the past to enable the fielder to decide how to move to catch this particular ball.

EP theory, on the other hand, eliminates the need to call information up from memory. When applied to baseball, EP proponents argue that the fielder does not need to rely on stored memory, but rather can make decisions based on information from OAC or LOT alone.

There is still a lot of discussion about which theory, if either, is more accurate for explaining how fielders judge fly balls. "This is still up for debate," noted Bleacher Report writer Dan Peterson, "as the IPers would argue 'learned facts' like what pitch was thrown, how a certain batter hits those pitches, how the prevailing wind will affect the ball, etc. And, with EP, how can the skill differences between a young ballplayer and an experienced major leaguer be accounted for? What is the point of practice, if the trials and errors are not stored/accessed in memory?"[21]

Regardless of which theory explains it best, there is no doubt that fielding the ball well includes a lot of aspects practice, skill, and science.

CHAPTER SEVEN

INNER SKILLS

Many people are passionate about baseball. Some focus on statistics, while others just take in the thrill of the game. Legendary baseball broadcaster Vin Scully retired in 2016 after 67 seasons calling games for the Los Angeles Dodgers. Perhaps more than anyone in the world, Scully knew baseball in a unique way. One thing he understood about baseball was time. He used long pauses in his broadcasts to let moments sink in, to bring gravity to the game he loved.

Time is a special thing in baseball. One famous thing Scully would say about outfielders involved all the waiting they'd have to endure between at bats, especially if their last one was a bad one. "That's the one thing about outfielders," he'd often say. "They have a lot of time to think and destroy themselves."[22]

The mental side of baseball is one of the most difficult things to understand about sports. Successful players can fall apart in the playoffs. Bats can go quiet. A single play can unravel an entire season. However, as the years have passed, people have learned more and more about the mental aspects of the untimed game. This has led to a better understanding of why baseball can take a psychological toll on all players.

Physical strength and skill are essential for succeeding at baseball, but they are not enough. Success in baseball also requires focus, confidence, and mental toughness—"inner" skills that cannot be coached. Psychologist Mike Stadler said, "Baseball is impossible without psychology: impossible to play, and impossible to appreciate fully as a fan."[23] Hall of

Fame pitcher Tom Seaver agreed. "The difference between the physical abilities of the players in the major leagues is not that great," he said, "and the difference between the teams is not that great. So what it comes down to is that the dividing factor between the team that wins and the one that loses is the mental attitude, the effort they give, the mental alertness that keeps them from making mental mistakes. The concentration and the dedication are the deciding factors."[24]

MANY VARIABLES

As noted, game of baseball has many moving parts. All positions in baseball require the ability to keep track of multiple variables at once, but this is especially true of the catcher. The catcher calls the pitches—in other words, they tell the pitcher which pitches to throw. Catchers do this by weighing a number of factors to determine which pitch has the best chance of striking the batter out, and they must be able to make this mental calculation very quickly. James R. Arkin and Robert M. Arkin, two scientists and baseball enthusiasts, explained:

> *[The catcher] must keep the score, the inning, and the number of outs in mind. He has to know what the count is and what the batter did the last time he was up to bat as well as in prior games. Is the pitcher's curveball working today? Does the umpire have a loose or a tight strike zone? Does the batter dig in? Is his weight leaning forward or on his heels? Do the runners have large leads, and which way are they leaning? … Each decision is crucial, because the outcome of the game could turn on any one.*[25]

According to the Arkins, the catcher's ability to make accurate decisions is based largely on a part of the brain called the medial prefrontal cortex hub. It processes social information—for instance, it is what gives people the ability to understand points of view that are different from their own. A key part of the catcher's job, the Arkins say, is encouraging the pitcher throughout the game, which can give them the confidence to make better throws. Since the catcher's calculations depend not only on numbers but also on the personalities and behaviors of

SPORTS PSYCHOLOGISTS

Psychologists are health professionals who help people work through various kinds of mental and emotional concerns, such as anxiety and stress. They may work in schools, in hospitals, in clinics, or for large companies. Although they are not medical doctors, they are highly trained in their field. In some states, a master's degree is required to become a psychologist, and in others, a doctoral degree is necessary. Psychologists must be licensed in the state in which they practice.

Sports psychologists specialize in working with athletes, especially those at the college, professional, and Olympic levels. They may work with a team or with an individual athlete. They may also be involved in research or teaching. Sports psychologists focus on helping the athlete achieve their maximum potential by building confidence, dealing with outside stresses, and coping with sudden success or failure. Research shows that sports psychologists can help injured athletes heal faster using techniques such as guided imagery—using the imagination to mentally "visualize" a desired outcome—and self-hypnosis.

Sports psychology is a growing field of study. An increasing number of colleges and universities have programs in the field, and an official professional organization, the Association for Applied Sports Psychology (AASP) offers certification in the field.

the other people on the field, the medial prefrontal cortex hub is crucial to their success.

THE BASEBALL PERSONALITY

What makes two players of comparable ability come to the major leagues and have very different experiences in terms of success? Stadler describes what he calls "the baseball personality," which can help answer this question. In 1980, the New York Mets drafted two players whose athletic abilities were similar—Daryl Strawberry and Billy Beane. When Strawberry began playing for the major league team in May 1983, he

Daryl Strawberry was a popular MLB player during the 1980s and 1990s.

struggled; by July, his batting average had dropped to below .200. Then one day, he came up to the plate in the eighth inning of a tie game. Despite his poor performance up to that point in the season and the high-pressure situation he found himself in, he did not doubt his ability. "I thought about hitting one out of the park and winning the game," he told reporters. That belief in himself paid off, and he did exactly what he had thought about doing. "I've always got the confidence," he told them. "I know I'm going to hit plenty more in situations like that."[26] He went on to hit 26 home runs that year and was named Rookie of the Year.

Beane, however, had a very different experience. Once in the major leagues, the pressure seemed to be too much for him, and his talent disappeared. In his book *Moneyball*, author Michael Lewis wrote, "Inside a batter's box he experienced a kind of claustrophobia. The batter's box was a cage designed to crush his spirit."[27] Beane's playing career lasted only six years and ended with a .219 batting average and only three home runs. Beane did not leave baseball for good, though. He became a successful general manager with the Oakland A's and helped bring about a statistical revolution in pro baseball. He never made an impact on the field, but Beane helped change how

ON BASE Baseball legend Joe DiMaggio was 18 years old in 1933 when he had a 61-game hitting streak for the minor league San Francisco Seals.

fans and teams value players and their abilities. His impact was just different.

A WINNING TEAM

Sometimes what seems to be a fantastic collection of players just can't click as a team. What makes a team work well together? Not all athletes are the same, and thankfully so. A group of individuals each full of the same amount of confidence and leadership qualities would make for a terrible team. How do athletes learn to work together to create a good team? "Do teams that succeed have a mix of leaders and followers?" Stadler asked. "Are successful teams made up of largely conscientious and responsible players? We need a study that asks 'All other things being equal, do teams with certain mixes of personality traits fare better than others?'"[28]

The way in which team members relate to each other and treat each other has been referred to as team chemistry. Good team chemistry means the team members work together to achieve a common goal, respect each other, and support each other even during times of failure or other stress. Research has suggested that team chemistry is related to a team's success on the field, and this would seem to make sense. If a group of people get along together, it follows that they would succeed more often. The reverse has also been shown to be somewhat true.

IN A SLUMP

Sometimes players have amazing streaks. From May 16 until July 17, 1941, New York Yankee Joe DiMaggio got at least 1 base hit in 56 consecutive games, the longest hitting streak in major league history. There have been more than 50 times when a player has had a hitting streak that lasted at least 30 games. Conversely, although not officially recorded, most players have experienced slumps—times when they may go several games and not get on base at all.

There are many variables at play during individual at bats, let alone during weeks or months-long hitting streaks. Confidence, concentration, and skill certainly play a part in hitting success, but it is more complicated than that.

"One potential problem," Stadler explained, "is that simply looking at whether or not an at bat resulted in a hit is to look past how well the ball was hit. A lazy infield pop-up and a line drive that knocks down the third baseman and breaks three bones in his glove hand both go into the scorebook as outs. A sizzling line drive up the middle and a bloop over the second baseman's head both [score] as hits. So ... the result depends to some extent on the quality of the contact ... and to some extent on luck."[29] Other factors—the defensive skill of the other team, the skill of the pitcher, the time of day or night, home game or away game—all play a role in a player's chances during any particular at bat.

Hitting slumps, though, may have more to do with psychological forces. Sometimes a player is not hitting well because of a mechanical problem with their swing or their stance. Other times, however, the player may be having trouble concentrating or remaining focused on the task at hand, especially if things going on in their life distract them from the game.

Joe Morgan, left, went through hitting slumps, but in 1990, he became a member of the Baseball Hall of Fame.

ON BASE Fans, often trying to snag a ball as a souvenir, have periodically interfered with MLB play. Some fans have even been banned from ballparks because of this.

Good players who are slumping may lose confidence in their abilities, and failure becomes even more likely as they start to believe that they have lost their skills. This depends a lot, though, on the players' attitudes—how much of the trouble they attribute to loss of skill and how much they decide is just bad luck. In 1983, a reporter for the *New York Times* asked Joe Morgan about his 0-for-35 hitting slump. "But I'm not in a slump," Morgan replied. "I'm just not getting base hits. There's a difference. A slump is when you're not hitting the ball and striking out. I've been hitting the ball; they're just making great catches."[30] Morgan kept his confidence in his abilities because he understood that sometimes, even when a player is doing well, the other team does better.

Getting out of a slump can be difficult for a ballplayer. However, today's game often focuses less on hits and batting average than ever before. A struggling player can be productive at the plate by working a walk or moving a runner along the bases. Study of mechanics, batting stances, or a pitcher's throwing can help players adjust and find a mental edge to get them out of a slump. Sports psychologists can also help.

AN ODD EFFECT

It's an odd psychological effect with an even odder name: "the yips." It is a term that causes terror in baseball players—so much so that many will not talk about it directly. When a player suffers from the yips, they have a mental hang-up that cannot allow them to complete a simple task. In baseball, that can be anything from a fielder unable to throw to a certain base, a catcher unable to throw back to a pitcher, or, in the worst cases, a pitcher suddenly unable to throw to the plate.

MLB pitcher Jon Lester dealt with the yips.

Charlie Maher, a sports psychologist, will not use the word "yips" to describe the ailment, instead insisting on the phrase "misplaced focus":

> *If their focus really is misplaced, it's on results … It's on what people are thinking. It gets them away from the fluidity of the process of the game. As a result, it snowballs. They start to judge themselves. They start to tense themselves up. The end result is that the ball is not going where it's supposed to go.*[31]

One famous modern example of the yips happened with St. Louis Cardinals pitcher Rick Ankiel in 2000. Ankiel suddenly lost the ability to throw strikes in the postseason, then lost all confidence in 2001. Ankiel spent years in the minor leagues trying to regain his confidence. Although he never pitched again, he completely rebuilt his career, and in 2014, he returned to the majors to play as an outfielder for the Cardinals.

Other players have also had to switch positions, or they have left baseball altogether. One example was pitcher Steve Blass, and because of his experience, the yips were sometimes referred to as "Steve Blass Disease." In the 1970s, Blass completely unraveled one year and retired from baseball at age 32. Chuck Knoblauch is another example: The second baseman suddenly lost the ability to throw to first base and had to become a left fielder. Beyond changing positions to avoid the mental hiccup causing the yips, there is little else known to help a player overcome the mysterious psychological ailment.

"Even if you knew exactly what caused your yips, what the heck do you do with it? It's just information,"[32] said Dr. Richard Crowley, who wrote a book about the phenomenon. Crowley said there is no real set of rules to help

Struggles with confidence can be fixed by team success, such as a World Series victory, as shown here.

ON BASE Many player superstitions involve eating. First baseman Justin Morneau had to eat the same sub before every game.

people overcome the yips, and little information available to explain what is happening inside a player's mind when it happens.

"There's no explanation on the planet to get over this," Crowley said. "When you're Superman and you get near kryptonite, you're beside yourself. You can't muster up all that stuff. All the information in the world cannot change a ballplayer who has this particular struggle."[33]

SUPERSTITION AND RITUAL

Fans and players alike often have superstitions and specific rituals around sports. Baseball in particular has a long and colorful history of superstitions. This may have something to do with the amount of time baseball players have to think about the game.

Superstitions are habits or routines people develop in an effort to gain control over something they cannot control through ordinary means. If a player has a good game, they may try to replicate the things they did before that game to reproduce the positive results for their next game. Third baseman Wade Boggs ate only fried chicken before his games. Houston Astros second baseman Craig Biggio never washed his batting helmet during the entire season. Pitcher Turk Wendell brushed his teeth and then chewed licorice between every inning. Some players refuse to step on the foul line as they take the field; others make a point of stepping on it. Many players feel an almost obsessive need to keep the same jersey numbers they have had since Little League.

One famous psychological research paper compared baseball players to a tribe of fisherman in New Guinea called the Trobriand. In George Gmelch's essay "Baseball Magic," he explained how the fishing habits of the Trobriand Islanders differ depending on where they fish. If they fish in the relative safety of a lagoon, the Trobriand require little religious ceremony or ritual before getting to work. Gmelch related this

Shota Imanaga of the Chicago Cubs threw a combined no-hitter in 2024. Many baseball superstitions have to do with no-hitters or perfect games.

to the habits of fielders in baseball, who often have little to no fielding rituals when they are working behind a pitcher. This is because, Gmelch proposes, fielding percentages are extremely high in the majors. Players are adept at computing the highly complex science that is necessary to catch a fly ball or complete difficult plays in the field. There is little uncertainty, and thus little help necessary from outside, unexplainable forces. Much like fishing in a lagoon in New Guinea, fielding behind the pitcher feels safe; there is little that can go wrong.

Ocean fishing, much like batting, is a much different story. Batters often deal in failure and can see long slumps without hits. There is danger lurking in the waters when facing a good pitcher, much like the chaos and uncertainty that comes with venturing out into the Pacific Ocean for food. "When fishing in the open sea," Gmelch wrote, "Trobrianders used a great deal of magical ritual to ensure safety and increase their catch."[34]

In baseball, batters and pitchers are constantly searching for ways to improve their game. To help them deal with the uncertainties of baseball, they create rituals—much to the frustration of their managers and the wonderment of those outside the clubhouse. They include batting routines, walk-up music, and other superstitious activities. When faced with uncertainty, both baseball players and tribal fisherman turn to magic for even a slight sense of added control. This is similar to the rituals created by people with obsessive-compulsive disorder (OCD), although for people with OCD, the rituals are not confined to one area of their lives. Additionally, people with OCD feel unable to control whether or not they perform their rituals. Having a superstition does not mean a player is mentally ill; they are simply trying to feel more in control of a situation that is mostly determined by luck.

The same goes for those outside of the game. For example, no one in the dugout will speak to a pitcher who is working on a no-hitter, or even talk about it, for fear of "jinxing" the pitcher. This idea of the jinx extends to fans in the stands, sportscasters, and even people watching on TV. Sports announcers may think that they might jinx a batter if they mention the hitting streak the batter is in at the moment, or they might jinx a pitcher by mentioning that the pitcher has not given up a home run in the last 10 starts.

Jinxes, curses, and superstitions are not proven by science. Both in baseball and in life, people control their own destiny. However, even knowing that, many think the right routine or habit can be the one thing that gives them an edge.

Superstitions or rituals can, in some ways, help players by giving them a sense of control over things. Despite that, there's no doubt that baseball is a game of science. Physics, biology, psychology, and more all play a part.

NOTES

Chapter One: A National Pastime

1. Quoted in Jon Bois, "There Is No Future of Baseball," SB Nation, March 29, 2017. www.sbnation.com/a/mlb-2017-season-preview/there-is-no-future-of-baseball.
2. Quoted in Mark Newman, "Why We Love Baseball," MLB.com, February 14, 2007. mlb.mlb.com/news/article.jsp?ymd=20070213&content_id=1800838&vkey=news_mlb&fext=.jsp&c_id=mlb.
3. Quoted in "10K Truth Baseball Quotes." www.10ktruth.com/the_quotes/baseball.htm.
4. Quoted in Richard Nordquist, "The Language of Baseball," About.com, 2009. grammar.about.com/od/words/a/baseballjargon.htm.

Chapter Two: The Physical Game

5. Jason R. Karp, "Muscle Fiber Types and Training," Coachr. www.coachr.org/fiber.htm.
6. Donald A. Chu, Jumping Into Plyometrics. Champaign, IL: Human Kinetics Publishers, Inc., 1998, p. 1.
7. Charles Slavik, "Training Differences of Baseball Players vs. Other Athletes," Coach John Peters' Baseball Tips. baseballtips.com/playertraining.html.

Chapter Three: Injury and Recovery

8. Quoted in "Orthopedic Experts Examine Baseball Throwing Injuries," *Medical News Today*, April 9, 2009. www.medicalnewstoday.com/articles/145703.php.
9. Quoted in "Smith Breaks Leg Sliding to a Base," *New York Times*, October 7, 1914. query.nytimes.com/gst/abstract.html?res=9A0CE5D71638E633A25754C0A9669D946596D6CF&scp=145&sq=October+7%2C+1914&st=p.

10. Quoted in "Orthopedic Experts Examine Baseball Throwing Injuries."

Chapter Four: Moving Parts

11. Quoted in Porter Johnson, "The Physics of Baseball," Illinois Institute of Technology. www.iit.edu/~johnsonp/smart00/lesson3.htm.
12. Quoted in Carl T. Hall, "A Neophyte Takes on the Science of Pitching," *San Francisco Chronicle*, July 9, 2007. articles.sfgate.com/2007-07-09/news/17253497_1_hitting-san-francisco-s-exploratorium-baseball-expert.
13. David Kagan, "The Physics of Radar Guns," *Hardball Times*, May 12, 2015. www.hardballtimes.com/the-physics-of-radar-guns.
14. Justin Arndt, "How Aroldis Chapman Threw the Fastest Pitch Ever," *Huffington Post*, August 28, 2016. www.huffingtonpost.com/entry/how-aroldis-chapman-threw-the-fastest-pitch-ever_us_57c38390e4b06384eb4066ef

Chapter Five: Hard Hitting

15. Quoted in "There's More Than Meets the Eye to Catching a Fly Ball in the Outfield," University of New Hampshire, April 10, 2006. www.unh.edu/news/news_releases/2006/april/lw_060410ball.html.
16. Quoted in Noel Wanner, "How Far Can You Hit One?: The Science of Baseball," Exploratorium. www.exploratorium.edu/baseball/howfar.html.

Chapter Six: Team Effort

17. Quoted in Harald Franzen, "Baseball Bat Cracks and Clunks Tell Outfielder Where to Go," *Scientific American*, June 11, 2001. www.scientificamerican.com/article.cfm?id=baseball-bat-cracks-and-c.
18. Quoted in "Crack! Clunk! Physicists—and Players—Tune in to the Sound of Baseball," The Free Library, May 6, 2002. www.thefreelibrary.com/Crack!+Clunk!+Physicists--and+players--tune+in+to+the+sounds+of...-a086170479.

19. Quoted in James Glanz, "The Crack of the Bat: Acoustics Takes on the Sounds of Baseball," *New York Times*, June 26, 2001. www.nytimes.com/2001/06/26/science/the-crack-of-the-bat-acoustics-takes-on-the-sound-of-baseball.html.
20. Mike Stadler, *The Psychology of Baseball: Inside the Mental Game of Major League Players*. New York, NY: Gotham, 2008, p. 54.
21. Dan Peterson, "Baseball Brains—Fielding into the World Series," Sports Are 80 Percent Mental, October 19, 2008. blog.80percentmental.com/2008/10/baseball-brains-fielding-into-world.html.

Chapter Seven: Inner Skills

22. Vin Scully's Twitter page, April 28, 2016. twitter.com/VinScullyTweet/status/725885893207199748.
23. Stadler, *The Psychology of Baseball*, p. x.
24. Quoted in H. A. Dorfman and Karl Kuehl, *The Mental Game of Baseball*. Lanham, MD: Diamond Communications, 1995, p. 1.
25. James R. Arkin and Robert M. Arkin, "Catching Science: The Mind Behind the Mask," *Association for Psychological Science*, vol. 25, no. 4, April 2012. sabr.org/research/catching-science-mind-behind-mask.
26. Quoted in Stadler, *The Psychology of Baseball*, p. 120.
27. Quoted in Stadler, *The Psychology of Baseball*, p. 120.
28. Quoted in Stadler, *The Psychology of Baseball*, p. 134.
29. Stadler, *The Psychology of Baseball*, p. 148.
30. Quoted in Dorfman and Kuehl, *The Mental Game of Baseball*, p. 217.
31. Quoted in Zack Meisel, "The Yips: Difficult to Understand, Difficult to Cure," MLB.com, May 10, 2013. m.mlb.com/news/article/47124896/the-yips-difficult-to-understand-difficult-to-cure/.
32. Quoted in Meisel, "The Yips."
33. Quoted in Meisel, "The Yips."
34. George Gmelch, "Baseball Magic," in *Magic, Witchcraft, and Religion: An Anthropological Study of the Supernatural*, ed. Pamela Moro. meissinger.com/uploads/3/4/9/1/34919185/gmelch_baseball_magic.pdf

GLOSSARY

ballistics: A method of training that maximizes power by applying a high amount of force to a low amount of weight and eliminates the need to expend energy by slowing and stopping the movement.

ballistic stretching: A method of stretching muscles that adds a series of small bounces to the stretch.

Bernoulli's principle: A principle of aerodynamics that states that the faster air moves over the surface of an object, the less pressure it places on the object.

concentric action: The phase of plyometric exercise during which the muscle contracts and applies its force.

conservation of momentum: A physical principle that states that momentum created in a moving object remains the same even when that momentum is transferred to another object.

dynamic stretching: A method of stretching muscles that includes moving through the joint's range of motion.

eccentric action: The pre-stretch phase of plyometric exercise during which the muscle builds and stores energy in preparation for contraction.

ecological psychology: A theory about human perception which states that human beings can make decisions based on information at hand without the need to call it up from memory.

elasticity: A physical property that describes how quickly the surface of an object returns to its original shape after being compressed.

electrolytes: Essential chemicals in the body that are necessary for the proper functioning of all the body's cells and systems.

fast-twitch fibers: Muscle fibers that contract more quickly and grow larger than slow-twitch fibers, but have less endurance.

force: Any outside stress that causes an object to move or change its shape.

force-velocity relationship: An equation used to measure power. Power equals force times distance divided by time.

friction: The resistance put on a moving object by a surface that causes it to slow down.

impingement: An overuse injury characterized by pressure placed on a nerve or blood vessel.

information processing theory: A theory of human perception that likens the brain to a computer that stores sensory input in memory for future use.

kinetic energy: The form of energy involved in movement.

linear optical trajectory: A theory of how a fielder judges the trajectory of a fly ball that is hit to one side rather than straight on.

Magnus force: The force on a spinning object that causes it to change its path in flight.

mass: The amount of matter contained in an object.

momentum: A measure of how an object moves, depending on its mass and velocity.

motor unit: The combination of a group of muscle fibers with the nerve that makes the muscle contract.

1RM: The maximum amount of weight that a person can move one time with a particular muscle.

optical acceleration cancellation: A theory of how fielders judge the trajectory of a fly ball that is hit directly toward them.

parabola: A mathematical curve that describes the shape of the trajectory of a fly ball. A parabolic curve is wider at its base than at its top, such as the arc of water coming out of a drinking fountain.

plyometrics: A method of power training that puts the muscles in a pre-stretch before executing a powerful contraction.

sequential summation of movement: A physics principle that states that conserved momentum transferred from a larger object to a smaller one will cause the smaller object to move faster than the larger object that provided the momentum.

slow-twitch fibers: Muscle fibers that contract more slowly and do not grow as large as fast-twitch fibers, but have more endurance.

static stretching: Stretching a muscle with a slow movement that is held in place for 20 to 30 seconds.

trajectory: The path followed by an object in flight.

trampoline effect: An action in which an object that is hit by another object becomes compressed, then springs back to its original form with minimal loss of energy.

velocity: A measure of the rate of change in position over a period of time in a particular direction.

FOR MORE INFORMATION

BOOKS

Braun, Eric. *Home Run: The Science Behind Baseball's Most Amazing Plays.* North Mankato, MN: Capstone Press, 2025.

Calcaterra, Craig. *Stars of Major League Baseball.* New York, NY: Abbeville Kids, 2023.

Clarke, David J. *Baseball Strategies.* Minneapolis, MN: SportsZone, 2024.

Harris, Beatrice. *STEM in Baseball.* Buffalo, NY: Cavendish Square Publishing, 2025.

Van, R. L. *Baseball: Then and Now.* Minneapolis, MN: Abdo and Daughters, 2024.

WEBSITES

Baseball Reference
baseball-reference.com
This website gives statistics and information about some of the most important players of the game.

The Exploratorium: The Science of Baseball
www.exploratorium.edu/baseball/
This brightly illustrated comic book-style website offers information about many aspects of baseball science.

How Stuff Works: How Baseball Works
entertainment.howstuffworks.com/baseball.htm
From the "How Stuff Works" series, this website includes videos and links to information about the game of baseball, including the equipment, rules, strategies for playing, and more.

The Science of Baseball
www.scientificamerican.com/report/baseball-science/
This website gives readers a wide variety of scientific articles about baseball, including ball physics and even making energy-efficient stadiums.

Society for American Baseball Research
sabr.org
This organization publishes research papers on the science of baseball.

INDEX

T

U

V

W

Y

PICTURE CREDITS

Cover, PeopleImages.com - Yuri A/Shutterstock.com; cover, pp. 1-104 hero mujahid/Shutterstock.com; cover, pp. 1,3, 4, 6, 10, 32, 44, 56, 67, 77, 87, 94, 96, 98, 103, 104 marooshka/Shutterstock.com; cover, pp. 1, 4-104 Free Icon Download/Shutterstock.com; p. 5 PeopleImages.com - Yuri A/Shutterstock.com; p. 8 WBMUL/Shutterstock.com; p. 10 https://en.m.wikipedia.org/wiki/File:Cy_young_pitching.jpg; p. 11 https://commons.wikimedia.org/wiki/File:1868_Reds.jpg; p. 13 https://commons.wikimedia.org/wiki/File:Babe_Ruth_by_Bain,_1919.jpg; p. 15 https://en.m.wikipedia.org/wiki/File:Jackie_Robinson_Kansas_City_Monarchs.jpg; p. 19 PeopleImages.com - Yuri A/Shutterstock.com; p. 21 https://en.wikipedia.org/wiki/File:Ty_Cobb_sliding2-edit1.jpg; p. 24 javi_indy/Shutterstock.com; p. 27 Mary A Lupo/Shutterstock.com; p. 30 leonori/Shutterstock.com; p. 33 Andrey_Popov/Shutterstock.com; p. 36 Maurice Savage / Alamy Stock Photo; p. 38 Conor P. Fitzgerald/Shutterstock.com; p. 41 Cal Sport Media / Alamy Stock Photo; p. 42 mTaira/Shutterstock.com; p. 45 https://commons.wikimedia.org/wiki/File:BE050522.jpg?uselang=ko; p. 48 https://commons.wikimedia.org/wiki/File:Fernando_Valenzuela_pitching,_1986.jpg; p. 49 Ozant/Shutterstock.com; p. 51 https://commons.wikimedia.org/wiki/File:Heinrich_Gustav_Magnus.jpg; p. 53 Jon Schulte/Shutterstock.com; p. 57 Everett Collection Historical / Alamy Stock Photo; p. 59 Kathy Hutchins/Shutterstock.com; p. 60 Prachaya Roekdeethaweesab/Shutterstock.com; p. 68 Super8/Shutterstock.com; p. 69 UPI / Alamy Stock Photo; p. 71 Irkhamster stock/Shutterstock.com; p. 73 Conor P. Fitzgerald/Shutterstock.com; pp. 80, 82, 84 ZUMA Press, Inc. / Alamy Stock Photo; p. 85 vnews/Shutterstock.com; p. 87 Xinhua / Alamy Stock Photo.

ABOUT THE AUTHOR

AMY B. ROGERS is an experienced nonfiction author who has written many books for young readers on topics that include American history, science, and women's participation in sports. She lives in a suburb of Buffalo, New York, with her husband, Steve, and their Welsh corgi, Jiminy.